UNPACKING THE BOXES OF OUR ATTACHMENTS

UNPACKING THE BOXES OF OUR ATTACHMENTS

**FREEING OUR TRUE
HAPPINESS WITHIN**

by
Randy Bell

Published by
McKee Learning Foundation

Copyright © 2014 by Randy Bell
All Rights Reserved
Printed in the United States of America

No part of this book may be
used or reproduced in any manner
whatsoever without written
permission except in the case
of brief quotations in critical articles
or reviews.

Cover Photo: "*Firebird*"
    Painting by Kathy Goodson   www.KathyGoodson.com
    Used by permission.

ISBN-13:   978-0-9895428-1-4

Published by
    McKee Learning Foundation
    3215 Baltimore Branch Road
    Hot Springs, NC   28743

For more information, contact:

    Info@McKeeLearningFoundation.com

    www.McKeeLearningFoundation.com

TABLE OF CONTENTS

Section   **Page**

1. Happiness And Unhappiness — 1
2. Seeking Happiness — 4
3. What Happiness Is — 6
4. Where Unhappiness Comes From — 8
5. Creating Attachments — 11

6. Looking Inside The Boxes Of Our Attachments — 16
   - Attachment To Tangible Things — 17
     - Accumulating Possession – "More Is Better" — 17
     - Creating Status Symbols — 19
     - Grass Is Always Greener — 21
     - A Story – "The Nutcracker" — 22

   - Attachment To Intangible Things — 25
     - Taught But Unproven Beliefs — 25
     - Refighting Past Battles — 28
     - Re-suffering Old Hurts — 30
     - Freezing The Moment — 32
     - Seeking Perfection, Faulting Others — 35
     - A Story – "It Must Be Perfect" — 37
     - Running From What Scares Us — 39
     - Lights, Camera, Action — 42

- Attachment To Perceptions of Self 46
  - Negativism And Intolerance 46
  - Defensive Strategies 47
  - Seeking Honors And Approbations 52
  - Riding The White Horse 55
  - Living To Satisfy Others 58
  - Adopting Roles 59
  - A Story – "Giving Away Your Life" 64
  - The Greatest Attachment 66

7. Distinguishing Wants From Attachments 69
8. The Journey To Unattached Living 73
9. Seeing Our Attachments 75
10. Unpacking The Boxes Of Our Attachments 84
11. Changing Our Attachments 88
12. Overcoming Resistances 96
13. Living Without Attachments 102
14. Author And Publications 105

****

"I believe the very purpose of our life is to seek happiness.
That is clear.

Whether one believes in religion or not,
whether one believes in this religion or that religion,
we all are seeking something better in life.

So, I think the very motion of our life is toward happiness."

(H.H. Dalai Lama)

1. HAPPINESS AND UNHAPPINESS

A car is driving down the highway at a high speed. Suddenly it darts into an adjacent lane, cutting off another driver who brakes to avoid a collision. Speeding another mile down the road, the car repeats its erratic move, cutting off a second car and causing that driver to also suddenly brake – along with several other trailing cars in sequence.

Consider the first threatened driver. Her good reactions applied the brakes quickly and firmly yet calmly. She took several deep breaths, and checked her mirrors to assure that other drivers were proceeding safely. She reminded herself to be sure to be especially vigilant on this highway as she continued her drive. She then quietly proceeded on her way without further consternation or disturbance.

Consider the second threatened driver. His slower reaction caused his car to more narrowly miss the offending driver. He hit his brake hard and swerved into the adjacent lane without knowing who might be there. As he continued with his drive, he vehemently cursed nonstop at the offending driver for his recklessness even though that driver was well out of earshot. And then he continued his rant and agitation time and again over the next several days as he related the story of this event, and his attendant grievances, to family and friends.

One event – a reckless cutting off of a car on a high-speed highway – happened to two different people producing two widely divergent reactions and states of mind. The first driver took note of the situation, responded calmly and smartly, quickly settled her emotions, and went about getting to her destination, leaving the incident behind her with minimal disturbance to her day. Her happiness with her life suffered only a small blip in her Life's journey as she reaffirmed to herself how lucky she was to be unscathed in her car, and to have been taught good defensive driving techniques.

The second driver lost himself within the situation of the moment, responded almost as erratically as the original offender, raised his anger to a peak pitch, and relived this disturbance over and over again long after the event. His unhappiness suffered a significant inflammation in his mental state as he reaffirmed to himself how dangerous Life can be even in the everyday act of simply driving your car.

When we are unhappy, particularly when our unhappiness has manifested itself as anger, our tendency is to look outward. We react to an external event, and blame people and circumstances for our unhappiness, with the assumption that the source of our unhappiness lies outside of us. Yet, as our driving example illustrates, happiness or unhappiness can easily arise out of the same event. The "event" (surrounding circumstances, life's conditions, hurtful words said, actions taken, etc.) is simply what it is, fixed in time and space and specifics. It does not recur – unless we choose to continually replay it in our mind or in conversations with others. It does not move – unless we carry it with us wherever we go. It does not change – unless we embroider or paint it differently with each retelling of it.

Whatever we may choose to do with that event, the event itself is inherently unchanged. But what the event means or signifies is personal, varying to each of us, dependent upon how we view it and elect to respond to it. Your response is likely to be very different than mine, even though we typically rationalize to ourselves that our response was "normal," a universal one. At least until we see someone responding differently, at which point we may think, "what is wrong with that person?" Or, in a very honest moment, we may think, "what is wrong with <u>me</u>?"

Which brings us to this most fundamental Truth about happiness: *happiness is a **relative** state based upon **our choice** to be happy or unhappy.* Being happy (or not) is a decision we make inside of us; it is not an external condition. No matter how rightly we may feel wronged; no matter how much we may see the world as a danger constantly conspiring against us; no matter how desperate are our circumstances; no matter how much we may chase the trappings that supposedly grant us happiness – career, family, things – happiness comes from the realization that it only comes from within us, not from outside of us. From how we choose to see, interpret, and live our lives. <u>We are happy simply by allowing ourselves to be so</u>.

"I am not what happens to me.
I am what I chose to be."
(C. J. Jung)

2. SEEKING HAPPINESS

"Most people are as happy
as they make up their minds to be."
(Abraham Lincoln)

All beings in all forms of life seek to be happy. To walk through the day with positive feelings and attitudes regarding what presents itself to us. To be confident rather than fearful. To feel safe rather than fearful. To be about the business of *doing* rather than worrying about the potential problems from trying to do. To live within a sense of calm rather than the stress of conflict. To have clarity about one's direction, rather than paralyzing confusion. To live today's life, not trying to escape the past or daydream the future. To have peace in the midst of all the surrounding chaos, rather than being the chaos itself.

But all too often, such happiness seems elusive, awaiting us "tomorrow" when things hopefully will be different. Happiness seems to be something we have to "get," something we have to make, a target for us to pursue, an end result to be achieved. Yet happiness is already here within us, trapped inside our distorted understandings of what happiness is supposed to be, waiting for us to allow it to be released and fully envelop us. The only one preventing our happiness is our own self.

In truth, we are continually building our own thick walls of unhappiness, shooting ourselves in the emotional foot, self-defeating our supposed efforts to be happy. "I have met the enemy, and it is us," as the character Pogo once said. It is only when we realize that the power of happiness lives within, held in our own hands rather than in the doings of others, that we have any chance of being happy. But first we have to stop making ourselves miserable. And stop creating the barriers to our living happily. *We need to commit to allowing ourselves to live in happiness.*

"I think to a large extent whether you suffer depends on how you respond to a given situation."
(H.H. 14th Dalai Lama)

3. WHAT HAPPINESS IS

We talk often with others about happiness, our desire for it, what we think will give us happiness. We think we know what happiness is – at least for ourselves. So why does it seem so elusive, always somewhere out in front of us?

Happiness eludes us because we do not really know what happiness is. True happiness is not a fleeting, temporary state. True happiness is constant, ever-present in our life. It is a way of being, not a way of getting. It is not a life without difficulty, without challenges; these things are inherently part of being human, living a human life. Rather, *happiness is being at peace with the life we have, what we have done, where we have come to. It is a calmness of unified mind and spirit that delights in our very being, regardless of the ups and downs of our daily life.* Happiness is being accepting of what we have done to be where we now are – even if we think there are some things we did that we should not have done or should have done differently, or we would prefer to be somewhere else than where we currently are.

> "Where you is is where you is,
> so make the best of your situation."
> (Colonel Potter character, *M*A*S*H*)

Happiness knows that there is more to come our way, that our life experiences are not done yet. If life brings us difficulties, we will face them as we have faced difficulties before; we know we can move through them and thereby arrive at a satisfying place. If life brings us ease, we will assimilate and enjoy it as we have assimilated ease before; we know we will move through it and also arrive at a satisfying place. Genuine happiness comes from <u>both</u> the difficulties and the ease of our lives, because both are part of the realities of life itself. And we are fortunate to be alive and living this life we have.

Happiness is not about what is around us. It is what is *within* us. Happiness comes from deciding how we will interpret whatever comes to us – whether we will choose to see it as "good" or "bad" based upon our experiences. Happiness is about how we *respond* to the things that come to us, not the thing itself. When we fully realize that happiness comes from within, then we realize that our happiness is already there. We have only to allow it to be. And since it is an inside quality, our happiness can go wherever we go. It is portable, not affixed. It is akin to our breath: always here, always replenishing, always nourishing us. It is not something we have to bring in. We only need to give ourselves permission to allow it to come out.

Happiness is being happy to be happy.

> "The secret of happiness consists
> not in getting what you want,
> but in wanting what we get."
> (Johann Goethe, German writer)

4. WHERE UNHAPPINESS COMES FROM

The good news for us in our continuous search for happiness is that our *un*happiness comes from one singular source. Out unhappiness is not from a lack of money, a lack of a rewarding job, a lack of a romantic partner, a lack of a new house or car, a lack of having a dream vacation, or a lack of recognition from others of our worth. It is not about a loved one dying, a sick child, a bad accident, an inadequate education, or the struggle to pay the bills. All of these kinds of issues are very real to us, and should not be trivialized. They are moments of sadness that make up part of our Life's journey. But they are not the real causes of our unhappiness. They are merely the symptoms. They fold themselves under an expansive umbrella that encompasses our disappointments, angers, hurts, frustrations, inadequacies, defensiveness, sadness, and grief – various forms of mental agitation – that can at times bring us to the point of virtual helplessness.

Rather, the real source of our unhappiness is that *we want what we do not have, or we want for things to be different than what they really are.* It is crossing those fine but very real lines among what we "Need" (those <u>fundamental</u> things we require to live in society and support ourselves), what we "Want" (those things we would *like* to have), and what we "Crave" (those things we *think* we "need," think we *must* have). They are lines between working to improve our lot in life and to enjoy our just rewards, versus a desperate and disproportional quest for external affirmation and a craving for gratification. It is our unwillingness to be content with and enjoy what we have, to accept the truth of what things really are, and to live in sync with that knowledge rather than in a state of denial, that move us away from our inherent happiness and into the false state of unhappiness. It is the continual, incessant pursuit of our cravings, only temporarily satisfied and never truly fulfilled, that keep our genuine happiness bottled up.

We excuse ourselves for endlessly chasing our cravings because we rationalize that those objects are universally desirable and are therefore appropriate for us as well. Of course we should want these things! We chase them tenaciously, often for no obvious reason or against any reasonableness. Yet each person has his/her own catalog of cravings; it is very personal to each of us. Your cravings are likely to be very different from mine; I may well care less about the things that you deem important to you. As with our reckless highway driver described previously, two different people can have two different responses and views regarding one common experience. The same item can be an absolute necessity for one, a nice-to-have for another, and of no interest to yet another.

Why do we have these cravings? Because of a deep-seeded sense that lives inside of us that we lack something that would make us whole. Somewhere in our past experience, we felt a loss of something important to us at that moment, an incompleteness, a denial of a perceived want. Over time, the intensity of that denial grew stronger, transforming the original want into a now-pressing craving that we *must* have. That experience, and our sense of it, and the conclusions we drew in that moment, continue to fester almost unknowingly in our minds. That is the real disturbance to our peace and tranquility, the source of our discontent, the drive for our replacement needs. But no amount of "things" will compensate for that original denial long forgotten, that continuous incompleteness. Our unhappiness today is but a mirror of our unhappiness of yesterdays. And that unhappiness, that incompleteness, drives us into a very false perspective and relationship with the world that now surrounds us.

So our genuine search for happiness has to begin inside. With honest and careful analysis of our values, ambitions, and what drives us. With identifying those cravings that seem to define and attract us, and determining why we have chosen those *particular* cravings as our basis for happiness. Then coming to an understanding as to why we refuse to turn loose our pursuit of them, even though they cause us such agitation to our peace of mind. Or why they seem so unsatisfactory so quickly if we do manage to temporarily attain them.

> "The real voyage of discovery
> consists not in seeking new landscapes
> but in having new eyes."
> (Marcel Proust, French novelist)

5. CREATING ATTACHMENTS

Happiness is a state of mind, an outcome of how we see, a result of our perception. So if the door to our happiness swings inward, not outward, what do we find when we open and walk through that door into our mind?

Boxes. Rows and rows of boxes, of all kinds and sizes. They are piled high with box stacked upon box, blocking our way from moving forward. And near the back of the room are the biggest boxes of all, each one marked "Especially Fragile, Handle With Care." Given this barrier wall of boxes, we can barely see to the farthest side of the room where the restful area of beauty and happiness waits to welcome us.

Into those biggest of boxes we have consigned each of our original feelings of lacking that we experienced. They are the hardest boxes to lift, and most difficult to move out of our way. Each of the boxes nearest us at the entranceway is filled with something our creative imagination has constructed to fill one part of our lacking that we feel inside. The boxes are the baggage of artificial constructs that we think will bring happiness to us, will be happiness itself. We stuffed each box with an illusion, a substitute version of our original lack. And then we attached ourselves firmly to that replacement need, and invested ourselves heavily in achieving it. Our largest unmet lackings are found in the bigger boxes; as the demands from those lackings grow over the years, the intensity of our attachment to our current "craving" will also be greater.

How do we create ties of deep *attachment* to our cravings? First, we select some "object" to be the replacement of our perceived need. An object can be almost anything: person, place, thing, group, animal, plant, emotion, event, honor, career, life role, status, skill or talent – virtually any noun that we can name. Then we do three things with that object:

1. We *project* our wishes and desires onto this object. In our minds, we make it into whatever we *desire* it to be, what we *require* it to be, rather than what it intrinsically truly is. In this projected and false version, we assume it will satisfy our underlying craving.

2. We then create our own *definition* and *interpretation* of that projected object, the substance of what it "is" in our redefined imagination. We define it in terms that are meaningful to us from our own life experiences, based upon what we have seen and interpreted at particular times in our life. Those interpretations may have little resemblance to what that object is truly about in scope and in details.

3. Once we have these false ideas securely implanted on the objects we select, we hold on tenaciously *(attachment)* to these illusions that we have created. No matter what other persons may tell us, no matter what our actual contrary experiences may be with this object, and no matter how often contrary experiences happen, we hold on to our false conceptions. If somehow something should happen which finally bursts the bubble of our illusion, no matter; we simply give up on that illusion and latch on to a next illusion to take its place.

> "We do not see things as they are;
> we see things as *we* are."
> (The Talmud)

This *projection*, *interpretation* and *attachment* to objects is how a mass of metal we call an automobile becomes a must-have status symbol. How a hoarder fills an apartment to overflowing. How a 4000 square foot four-bedroom home comes to define the <u>minimum</u> housing requirement for two people. How a person sits in a well-paying job that they truly hate. How the seemingly "perfect marriage / perfect family" dissolves within an extra-marital affair or a runaway child – an inevitability that everyone else saw coming. How a dream vacation becomes an impossible credit card debt.

That is what is in those myriad boxes. The projected objects and the interpretation of them that we have created in our mind. Each box neatly stores and tightly protects its individual object, safe from destruction, sitting within our mental warehouse next to all the other boxes, ready to be pulled out on demand as needed.

It is a seemingly never-ending process of chasing what we do not have. We carry multiple false objects around in our mind, jumping around back and forth among them from moment to moment, convinced with certainty that "we know what we want." All the while we wear ourselves into exhaustion trying to keep up the chase for our many cravings while maintaining the façade of our life. What we refuse to see and acknowledge is that it is not about actually *obtaining* the object of our need; it is about *the chase itself* – which is why it is unending.

Until that day comes when we run out of steam. The energy required for the chase finally exceeds our stamina. Our illusion falls apart with such staggering vehemence that we can no longer deny that what we have wanted, what we have believed, is untrue. What we have hung our hats on, what has defined us, what has fueled us all of this time, has been a lie. A self-made lie. We are then left groundless, confused; we only know that what has seemingly worked before now no longer works for us. Thankfully, the fog of our self-deception has been lifted. But what we now see is unfamiliar, unrecognizable, perhaps even frightening. We just know we can no longer proceed as we have been moving previously. But where do we go next?

That is the critical question. We can choose to retreat, go back into that warehouse and bring out yet another box, or create a new illusion packed into a new box, and proceed on our way once again. Even though one small part of us will know that our world has been irrevocably changed, however much we may try to deny it to ourselves and to others. Or we can begin to unpack this revealed box. We can even commit to starting to open other boxes that sit in our mental warehouse. Pull out more of those false objects, expose them to the warm breath of fresh air, and then consign them to the dumpster.

Most of us will not start that unpacking work, beyond maybe one box Life has forced us to now open in this immediate moment. The boxes are too many, the job is too hard, the contents are too scary, the potential empty warehouse looks too barren. It is like walking into an empty house. For many people, trying to imagine new "stuff" moved into there, and what their future life might look like in this new house in the midst of such current emptiness, cannot be envisioned. For some others, decorating this empty house with wholly new furnishings, creating a new home and a new life, is simply an opportunity too good to pass up.

This is where happiness begins. With the unpacking of our boxes of created objects. As anyone knows who has had to empty out an attic, move to a smaller house, close out a parent's home, or leave a house due to a divorce, all those possessions inside have many memories, so we likely have strong attachments to the objects we encounter. Letting loose of them, sending personal treasures to Goodwill, holding the yard sale, is not easy emotionally. The giving away, the letting go, the cutting of those attachments can be very difficult. But we manage to do it, either because we just have to do it, or because we believe that something better awaits us afterwards. Gradually, the overstuffed chair just becomes a chair again, not the warm, secure place where you nestled into your father's lap for comfort when you were hurting. And the family photos become just a reminder of good times and good people now past, not a model of a former life to be artificially recreated in current times.

Our packed up objects return to their true state, to be only what they originally were before we overly adorned them. Our attachments to them are gradually snipped away. With each box unpacked, we feel an incredible weight being lifted, a return of our energy, a calmness in our mind. And we make note … this is what happiness is really about.

> "We can never obtain peace in the outer world
> until we make peace with ourselves."
> (H.H. Dalai Lama)

6. LOOKING INSIDE THE BOXES OF OUR ATTACHMENTS

The first step in beginning to open these boxes of our distorted objects, and disconnect our unhealthy attachments to them, is to see what our own personal attachments are. This is a more difficult step than it may sound at the beginning of our efforts. Our initial objects – ambition, reward structures, protective barriers around our self – were likely created long ago and have been continually added to ever since. Over time, our attachments to them have continued to grow in intensity and believability, especially as we have found occasions to repeatedly reinforce them. By this time we are barely conscious of them; they are second nature to us, thoroughly infused into our thought processes and reactions. They have, in fact, come to define "me" – my values, my opinions, my view of the world, my personality, the very essence of "me." And, proving the depth of my attachments to these things, I will fight with all my strength to defend that evolved definition of my Self. It is another way we exhaust ourselves as a result of our attachment to objects: our constant defense of, and attachment to, this false self. But in our hearts, we know we are seeking to defend the indefensible.

So we have to take that first step, surmount that first big hurdle: confronting our self, identifying and acknowledging the objects we have created, and seeing how our attachments play out in our daily living. This is a completely personal exercise. Friends and family may perhaps be of some help in this process by pointing out areas where we may demonstrate impatience, excessive stubbornness, short temper, oversized ambitions unrealistic for our circumstances. Where we are overly critical of others, defensive at slightest criticism, unwilling to be open to suggestions, negative about the future, obsessive about doing tasks in a particular way, etc. These traits may or may not prove to be clues as to where we may have created artificial cravings for ourselves. But only you can ultimately determine if the clues take you to a dead end, or to an opening of personal discovery.

Once we begin to follow these clues, how do we then recognize our objects and our attachment to them? What do some objects and their attachments look like? Let us examine a few categories of such examples.

ATTACHMENT TO TANGIBLE THINGS

Accumulating Possessions – "More Is Better"
Under this heading, the Attachment is to the Quantity of Things. The objects can be from many different choices appropriate to us: souvenirs, collectibles, home furnishings, kitchen devices, Facebook friends, articles of clothing, etc. Though we may talk glowingly about each item (object) we are accumulating, each really carries minimal value to it. The intention is simply to amass numbers. If the hole of incompleteness within us is especially large, we then operate with the sense that great quantity is required to fill such a gapping void in our being. So we buy, we accumulate, we store, we hoard. We may even require more space to handle the quantity – hence the garage with no cars, the basement no longer a rec room, the added backyard storage locker.

The potential objects? The closet that overflows with clothes, including the 1000+ shoes. The "collectibles" hobbyist, stuffing things onto shelves and cabinets so densely that each individual piece goes unnoticed amidst the clutter. The "bragging right" is not about the special characteristic of individual items, but on the total quantity in the collection.

Food attachments frequently fall under this category. The objects can take on many forms: the total intake of food; the type of food excessively eaten (often the sweet, rich foods as "rewards"); a cultural emphasis to hold on to one's heritage identity; a full plate of anything to stave off feared hunger or starvation; the overflowing buffet table at party times to demonstrate hospitality skills. In *attachment*, the food in the pantry and refrigerator is disconnected from the weight on the scale or the size of the guest list.

The yardstick for how many antiques, bric-a-brac, kitchen gadgets, bottles of wine, paintings, or rooms are required to make a house into an attractive and comfortable home for its occupants becomes a bloated, always increasing number. Our sense about how much more money over and above our living requirements is really needed to make us happy becomes clouded. Our desire for quantity may drive us to have "all" of any one kind of object, or many kinds of different objects instead. Will the one with the most toys really win?

The clue to this attachment is that we buy not just a little more, or to accommodate a specific requirement, but that we buy well beyond what is functionally required. Certainly shopping is a necessary task if we are to feed, clothe, and house ourselves and our families. Shopping can also be recreational, and an outlet for our creative energies. But when we struggle to turn down a "sale" item; or to walk out of a store empty-handed; or are nervously discomforted by a bare sliver of space in our bookcase; or our shopping is a mindless, disconnected walk through the aisles; or resulting credit card debt threatens our financial well-being; then that kind of shopping does not bring us happiness. All that quantity does not fill the void in our hearts. Everything we see simply reminds us of the missing things we do not see, and must obtain. Quantity only reinforces the unhappiness we are seeking to escape.

"Trying to be happy by accumulating possessions
is like trying to satisfy hunger
by taping sandwiches all over your body."
(George Carlin, comedian)

Creating Status Symbols
Under this heading, the Attachment is to <u>Added Value</u>. Projecting a false meaning and value to an object beyond its intrinsic definition. Status attachment is closely related to the Attachment of Quantity of Things. If we believe that we are "less than," that we live beneath the levels of others, or we feel we are a failure in our pursuits, then our need is to change the perception others have of us. If they only see our failures, cannot see the good that we are, then we may seek to give them better, more visible yardsticks by which to measure us. It is once again about accumulating, but our accumulation is not for quantity; it is for perceived "quality." If the objects that surround us are of quality, then (the thinking goes) it must be that we ourselves are of quality. The potential flaw here is that we accumulate what *we* judge as quality. But quality is based upon "taste," and taste is an individual, relative thing. Others might well not see the quality we presume in the objects we select; one person's taste is another person's tacky. That misconnection creates yet another variation of unsatisfying craving.

The potential objects? The house, built in just the "right" location, constructed with all expensive, top-of-the-line products. The chef-grade commercial kitchen for the couple that rarely cooks or entertains. The designer fine arts and crafts in the bookcase. A brand-new, expensive car always in the driveway.

Food can once again service this kind of attachment. Dining out solely at expensive 4-5 star restaurants. Only imported, gourmet food in the pantry. Wines from top regions and wineries. Serving accoutrements in the kitchen purchased from top cooking stores.

Expensive vacations and top-flight hotels. First class travel, not coach. Clothes and accessories from the top fashion houses. Front row theater seats. The glamor careers and status professions that we select. The list can be endless, almost whatever the human imagination can mentally conceive.

It is not that these items, and the ownership of them, are inherently a bad thing. Being a patron of the arts, a supporter of creative artisans, can be commendable. Enjoying special and unique things can give us joyful moments. If one's wealth comfortably allows for such indulgences, there is no inherent harm in availing one's self of them.

The evidence of this attachment is not that we have our status symbols or that we enjoy them. It is what happens to our self-confidence when we cannot obtain them anymore, or lose the ones we have. It is when we forget how to enjoy simpler things when they arise, and feel we must ONLY partake of "the finer things." (Can a millionaire comfortably eat a slice of pizza, with her hands?) It is when we forget that there are other ways of living occurring each day that can also be fully satisfying in people's lives. It is when we are continually panicked at the thought that "the good life" might suddenly disappear from our grasp.

Attachment is when we think that, without these external status symbols, we have no positive status. That our status is defined by *what* we have rather than *who* we are. Happiness does not come from having our status symbols. Their constant presence in our life continually reminds us of the status that we feel we lack.

Grass Is Always Greener
Under this heading, the Attachment is to <u>Lacking</u>. We see things (objects) that we do not have. Our predominant thought is not really of the object itself, or its real value (or not) in our life, but only that we do not have it. And someone else does.

In Biblical terms, we lust, we covet, our neighbor's good fortune. There is not really a serious effort to actually *obtain* that object for ourselves; that would simply negate the attachment to the craving. We may even have a similar version of the object we covet, but we perceive it as an inferior, lesser one. The attachment is to the lacking, the not having. "Not having" affirms the profound misery and suffering of our life.

As with other attachments, the selected object can be almost anything. Person A sees Neighbor B with a new car every year, while Person A always has to drive a second-hand used one. Yet Neighbor B envies the fact that Person A is able to pay off his car loan and enjoy the luxury of no car payment. Person C sees Neighbor D completely remodeling her old kitchen, while Person C continues cooking meals on her old stove. Yet Neighbor D, standing in the middle of her wrecked kitchen, envies the fact that Person C is lucky not to have to be managing this disruptive, costly project and enduring the emotional toll it is taking. Person A sees Neighbor B taking regular family vacations in Europe, while Person A is only able to spend every summer at a state park campground in the nearby mountains. Yet Neighbor B envies the fact that Person A is able to stay close to home and enjoy a genuinely restful break rather than absorbing the draining chaos of foreign travel. Person C sees Neighbor D able to be a stay-at-home mom while Person C has to work to make ends meet. Yet Neighbor D envies the fact that Person C is able to get out of the house and enjoy a career while Neighbor D is "stuck at home." Person A sees Neighbor B having been able to retire early and now having all this free time to enjoy, while Person A expects to have to still work for many more years. Yet Neighbor B envies the fact that Person A still has a job to go to and colleagues to work with, rather than now sitting at home bored to death with no idea what to do with himself.

The evidence of this attachment is not just that we crave what we do not have, but that someone else does have it, and we do not, so their life is "better." Our jealousy even sadly prevents us from fully enjoying and sharing the good fortune of others. Even if they are good friends or family, our need to covet blinds us to what their perspective may be about their good fortune. As illustrated above, if others have their own Grass Is Greener attachments, then an expanding linked chain of attachments can ripple through an interlaced network of family, friends, neighbors, and communities. Or even among nations.

Being inspired by the accomplishments of others can be ennobling and motivating. But when clouded by our own feelings of inadequacy, consumed by the belief that "others have it better," such accomplishments do not spur true motivation and drive. The drive to "have what they have" immobilizes us in defeatism, leads us down an unending chase, traps us in our unhappiness.

> "Thou shalt not covet thy neighbor's house;
> thou shalt not covet thy neighbor's wife,
> nor his man-servant, nor his maid-servant,
> nor his ox, nor his ass,
> nor any thing that is thy neighbor's."
> (Torah, Exodus 20:13)

A Story – "The Nutcrackers"
One Christmas season, I attended a Christmas Candlelight House Tour where people open their homes and share their decorations of the holiday season. For this, I opted to visit a Revolutionary War-period town in South Carolina which had a number of traditional

homes on display. Entering the first house on the tour, the owner extended a cheery welcome as we entered into the front hallway.

If you could call it "entering." Once inside the house, people could barely move. Not because of the congestion from all the visitors, but from the overwhelming onslaught of the many decorations upon our eyes. Besides the large, highly-decorated natural Christmas tree in the front parlor, every room was filled with giant-sized Christmas balls, ballerina and Santa Claus figurines, and plastic Christmas trees of all various sizes scattered about. But the obvious focus of the owner's presentation was her collection of wooden nutcracker characters of all types and sizes displayed throughout each room. Then came the centerpiece of the exhibit – one entire room dedicated to these nutcrackers, filling the shelves behind the glass cabinet doors with seemingly no inch of space left for yet one more figure. I could not begin to imagine the total count nor the money spent to build this collection. It was a volume of collection that could have easily been shared for great joy in the schools, public buildings and library of this small community.

In her attempt to show her guests "everything," the conglomeration of it all meant that you effectively saw nothing. Our eyes simply glazed over from the sheer volume of the displays, creating a kind of visual claustrophobia. Each individual nutcracker was lost in the visual cacophony of the presentation. The scene was reminiscent of numerous Christmas mornings with presents strewn across the floor, one unwrapping rapidly after another, such that each individual gift loses its meaning and its specialness.

If our host's goal was to infuse us with the festive spirit of the season, the opposite effect occurred. The garishness and gluttony of the season was reinforced instead. The quality of any individual nutcracker, the specialness of its construction and craftsmanship, the uniqueness of its character, was not allowed to be seen. Those qualities were all sacrificed to quantity as people struggled to make their way through the house to exit through the back door.

I do not know the homeowner personally, so I cannot say with any accuracy what drives her to feed this continually-expanding collection. But the extreme number strongly suggests an attachment to quantity that has well lost sight of proportion, focused not on the spirit of Christmas giving but on the spirit of personal status. A status of quantity; a status of outdoing others; an attachment to "more." It simply left one wondering: what was her perceived shortcomings in her Christmases past that this collection is trying to make up for now?

ATTACHMENT TO INTANGIBLE THINGS

Taught But Unproven Beliefs
Under this heading, the Attachment is to our Personal Values and Beliefs. As children, we are taught that we should have "values," certain strong and fundamental beliefs and ways of acting that shape our character and define who we are. Even more, we are also told what those specific values and beliefs are to be. For many parents, such teaching is a fundamental charge of their child-rearing responsibilities. It is a charge also taken on by an endless variety of schoolteachers, clergy, employment supervisors, and other substitute parents. The child, seen as a "blank slate to be written upon," takes it all in as unquestioned truth from knowledgeable authorities. Unquestioned because questioning is not given an encouraging welcome, and a personal baseline of beliefs has not yet been established.

So the child, the adolescent, and even the adult accepts these truths. Each truth becomes a value, and each value becomes an intangible object – attached to as tightly as one affixes to any tangible object. The boy is taught what it means to be "a Southern gentleman." The girl is taught how to be "a proper lady." The religious clergy teach the commandments, the rules of spiritual behavior required to access God's Heaven and to avoid God's wrath. The schools teach the responsibilities of good citizenship. Sports programs teach the necessity for good teamwork. The job teaches the rewards from working hard and performing well. The courts teach what conduct is appropriate to live in a society of community.

All of this teaching yields values upon values. But most of this teaching is a one-way direction. Rarely does anyone stop to ask the listener, "What do *you* think?" In the minds of most of these teachers, the thought does not even arise to ask such a question of so blank a mind. And in the onslaught of so many teachings from so many teachers, it may not even occur to the student to be asked.

So the values and beliefs of others are simply pasted onto the child, offered without counter-perspective, and with no "proof" of veracity experienced by the child. Hence the taught values and beliefs create false understandings because they are based upon the teacher's own incomplete views of Life. These imposed values thereafter simply become "my" values and beliefs without self-reflection. And so those values and beliefs become more definitions of "me." The harder we may try to cover over this illusion of our Self, and the shakier our inner confidence is in those beliefs, the more we may exaggerate our absolute faith in them. "This is me, like it or not," or "this is who I am, take it or leave it" becomes our mantra, leading to "in your face" difficult personalities.

But if our life travels take us to different environs, or we have a life-changing personal event that does not fit with our past beliefs and expectations, or in some other manner we become exposed to different perspectives and experiences, in our heart nagging questions begin to arise. Are those original teachings we heard correct? Are those ideas true? Is this really "me"? If we begin to have our doubts of these truths, however unsaid those doubts, the foundation for our values weakens. That weakness can take us in several directions. We can make each value another one of our objects, packed in its own box, and defend it at all costs. We can fiercely defend both the value itself as true, as well as its status as "my value." Or if the pressure of our doubts accumulates until finally boiling over, we may suddenly lurch our life in a different direction, announcing in our renunciation that we "need to go find our self." Because the self we thought we were may not be the real self we are.

In the first case, the defensive posture, we become consistent and rigid in our beliefs. There is nothing new to learn. Our teachers are still to be honored and their teachings accepted. We become a bastion of stability in the face of surrounding change and counterarguments. We also likely locate ourselves with a similar looking, and a common thinking, homogeneous community that will continuously reinforce our perspectives of truth and values. Travel to culturally different locales, whether at home or abroad, is infrequent; if temporarily transported, we will reinterpret and translate what we see back into our normal forms of reference, glossing over or discounting intrinsic differences. ("We don't do it this way in America!")

In the second case, the offensive posture, we become changing and flexible in our beliefs. Many things are to be learned anew. Old teachers and their teachings are rejected, perhaps seen as traitors to our upbringing; new teachers and teachings are found to replace them. We float through various new experiences, often moving from one teacher to the next in continual search for "the new right answer." There is a somewhat wander-lust, ungrounded sense to it all, constantly seeking out what is different. Exploring new locations, finding different friends of other cultures, delving into new thoughts. The mind remains continually unsettled.

Attachment lives in both of these worlds. Unquestioned attachment to the old stunts our spiritual and intellectual growth, perpetuates a false definition of self not of our own making, and raises fears of having our beliefs challenged and their weaknesses exposed. Attaching to a chase for the new skips over a critical examination of the old and retention of that which is still good, still relevant. Blind acceptance just because it is new and different precludes critical discernment, and simply replicates "taking other people's word for it." Whether an old belief or a new belief, uninformed, untested, and unproven opinions betray our human capacity "to decide."

In the late 1960s, I was in a social gathering with friends when the conversation turned to the recent destructive race riots in Detroit.

People spoke freely and judgmentally about their condemnation of the Black rioters, and what an affront the violence was to "civil order" and "American values." Finally, I asked the group: "Have any of you ever been to Detroit? Have any of you seen the conditions in which the Black community lives?" No one had. There was an immediate awareness that all of these sanctimonious opinions were not built upon full experiential information, but rather just limited perspective from no first-hand contact. The conditions in Detroit held no resemblance whatsoever to the conditions in our homogeneous small southern city that my friends all knew. In Detroit, the world looked very differently. It can be very easy to build beliefs based upon conceptual ideas that have had no contact with experiential reality. It is through our own experiences, combined with unprejudiced reasoning, that actual knowledge is created.

Attachment to old beliefs typically cause the digging in of heels, reflexively rejecting other alternative values and beliefs, often leading to conducting personal attacks on people espousing those alternatives. The hard truth is, attachment to our beliefs, our certainty that we see and know things correctly, can be the <u>hardest, most painful attachments to give up</u>. Attachment to new beliefs often causes values and beliefs to change frequently, based upon the last opinion expressed; the result is little depth to one's beliefs. A tenacious attachment to a new belief is as big a trap as an attachment to old beliefs. A kneejerk rejection of old beliefs is as big a trap as a kneejerk rejection of new beliefs. Both lead us to a continuing unhappiness drawn from ignorance.

> "Am I a person of strong opinions but no ideas?"
> (anonymous)

Refighting Past Battles
Under this heading, the Attachment is to <u>Reversing Old Defeats</u>. Conflicts are a normal part of living. Any two people have

somewhat different beliefs, needs and wants, ambitions, background and experiences. So it is probable, if not inevitable, that conflicts will arise, especially if one is in a social or physical power position over the other. Conflicts arise in personal relationships, parent/child relationships, job relationships, societal relationships, and with everyday service providers we encounter as we go about our daily tasks. We will "win" some of these conflicts, and our beliefs and desires and ambitions will move forward. But the reality is that we will also "lose" many of our conflicts. Our beliefs and objectives will then be thwarted from moving forward. How important our beliefs or objectives were to us will then dictate the strength of our reaction to that loss.

If the depth of our attachment was slight, we will mentally let go of the argument easily and file it in the "win some, lose some" box. But if our attachment was great and built upon one of our other significant attachments, or we question the victor's motives or ethical conduct in the winning of the conflict, then the battle itself will become the issue over and above our original attachment. The conflict, the fight, becomes yet another object in our warehouse, and we become deeply attached to the perceived injustice of our loss.

So we replay that battle over and over again in our mind. We think of all the things we should have said in the moment of conflict: the snappy comeback that eluded us; the pertinent element of fact that went unmentioned; the line of convincing, indisputable reasoning that went unoffered. We consciously believe that we are angry at the other person's conduct and the fact that they won the battle. But in truth we are equally (or more) angry at ourselves for *losing* the battle, for our inability to keep up in the match of wits, at our lesser position that required deferring to the winner. It is even more painful if circumstances subsequently showed that our argument was the correct one, in which case "I told you so" is added to the depth of our frustration. We continually recall this battle, replay it in our minds, and retell it to friends and family repeatedly.

In some instances when we are not overly attached to this event, we may actually learn constructive insights and techniques from this loss, useful in future similar circumstances that might arise. But in attachment, we see only the loss and the need to rewrite this script in our minds – a script in which <u>we *always* win</u>.

But in truth we did not win. No matter how many times we revise and replay the story, the bitter truth is that *we will never change the original outcome*. Out antagonist has long since moved on, secure in his/her victory, the battle long forgotten. We are the ones stuck in past time, living the fantasy of our imagined victory. The fantasy may give us a momentary satisfaction as we replay our revised script once again, but the reality sets back in quickly. Indulging the fantasy only reminds us once again of our loss. And the biggest irony is that each time we refight the battle and pretend to win, when reality returns the real winner beats us once again! By re-trying to win, we re-lose time and time again.

It is not the winner that makes us unhappy. It is our own decision to attach ourselves to the conflict that stymies us and brings us our unhappiness.

> "Hanging onto to resentment is letting someone
> you despise live rent-free in your head."
> (Ann Landers, advice columnist)

<u>Re-suffering Old Hurts</u>
Under this heading, the Attachment is to our <u>Suffering and Martyrdom</u>. This attachment is similar to Refighting Past Battles. It is latching on to a past event of feeling hurt or injured, emotionally and/or physically, and keeping it continually alive in current time. It is another script that we replay, except that it is the

original script, not a rewritten one, unchanged except perhaps for some added ornamentation and intensity. And we do not "win" in this retelling; we forever continue to lose in each recurrence.

Perhaps someone: said something insensitive to us; did something mean to us; did *not* do what we expected of them (or they promised they would do); let us down; rejected us; disappeared in our moment of need. It is the pain of divorce; of a parent's scolding; of playground bullying; of criticism of our conduct; of deprecation of our talents or worth. In the extreme, it is mental abuse; physical violence; the moment illness or death struck.

We make this event into a defining moment in our life, a point from which our life took a turn – however great or slight. The greater our insecurity or vulnerability in that moment is the greater our pain or anger, and thereby the greater our attachment to that moment. Another player, "the perpetrator," is usually part of our hurt, and we will be quick to identify them as "the cause" of our hurt. But what we are really focused on is the hurt itself, its unfairness, and the legitimacy of our suffering.

Our response may be to wallow in that hurt, never finding a resolution or counteraction to it. Or we may seemingly move ourselves forward in some manner – pick up the pieces from our divorce, change our conduct to stop the bullying, tune out the criticism, apologize and supposedly "forgive" the perpetrator. If these are not genuine actions, done in spite of the hurt, then we risk ennobling ourselves and drifting into a kind of martyrdom. Our attachment now becomes to preserve our nobility achieved by having lived through the event, risen above the hurt.

But in fact we have not moved on. We come back to our hurt constantly in our mind and in our conversations. We continue to look for sympathy from others, expecting that they will reaffirm the rightness (righteousness) of our pain and subsequent suffering, and the wrongness of the perpetrator's action. ("You poor dear.")

We work hard to retain the pretense of our nobility in the face of such ill treatment. Or we shut down and turn away from the pain and the reminders of it. We sit on the couch complaining about the unfairness of our pain, unable to build a new life for ourselves. We feel defeated in attempting something new even before we start it. We may say we forgive, but we resent good things that subsequently come to our perpetrator, and (quietly) rejoice in his/her misfortunes, and continue to judge the ongoing actions of his/her life. This is how we drift into becoming "the perpetual victim" – destined to be continually treated wrongly, thereby expecting the world to provide us an apology and special compensatory treatment.

Our suffering from this pain is now a major reason for our being, our primary story to tell; there are few new stories to tell about our life. Attaching to old hurts takes us off the hook from taking on new Life experiences – such new experiences are seen as probable new pains. These past hurts are usually the bigger, stronger boxes, able to keep out the shocks of future new pains. We are seemingly happy in our unhappiness. Opportunities for real happiness pass us by while we remain mired in attachment to our unhappiness.

> "The conflict between what one is and
> what one expected to be touches all of us.
> And sometimes, rather than reach for what one could be,
> we choose the comfort of the failed role,
> preferring to be the victim of circumstance,
> the person who didn't have a chance."
> (Merle Shain)

Freezing the Moment
Under this heading, the Attachment is to <u>A Moment In Time</u>. We encounter many different experiences at various points in our lives. Some we remember fondly, with great joy, bringing us great satisfaction. Some we remember not so fondly, with great sadness,

leaving us highly dissatisfied. In either case, these are moments which had a significant, if not profound, impact on us. An impact which has conditioned our thinking and actions ever since.

In attachment we go beyond just memories, and continually strive to go back and reclaim those moments. We try to relive past moments of glory; the thrill of victory; the sound of applause; the warmth of a romantic episode; the prideful event for our child; the vacation to a seeming paradise. We try to re-experience those fleeting events, but to no avail: they were a one-time single circumstance now gone. Yet we nevertheless try to push current circumstances, people and places into that memory, remold them into what they are not, and pretend that "now" is really "then." Yet the fantasy is difficult to admit or to give up. But "then" is not, can not, and should not be "now."

With our not-so-happy moments, we still freeze them in time, and (surprisingly) return to them also. But in this case it is not to relive, but to rewrite. We fill our thoughts with "if I had just done this instead ..." thinking that in our rewriting efforts we can somehow change that moment, or at least our perception of it. The accident that would not have happened; the child that would not have failed; the hurtful words that would not have been said; the spouse that would not have walked out the door. We believe that somehow a different involvement or intervention from us would have stopped the damage.

Related to the Attachment to A Moment In Time is an attachment to a moment of failure. A failure that wounded deeply. But rather than wallow in it or plead for continual sympathy from the world at large, we take a more aggressive counteraction. We revisit the failure, but we rewrite the script onto a fresh substitute player, thinking that through them we can transform the memory of the failure into a success. Hence the failed actress becomes the iconic pushy stage mother dragging her child from one audition to the next. The failed ball player becomes the overly-aggressive Little

League coach screaming at his young charges, trying to exhort them into professional level playing standards. The failed entertainer or artist becomes the obsessive manager dominating his protégé. These are two-player dominate/submissive relationships, unhealthy and unhappy for both, always destined to collapse at some key future juncture.

We understand that the moment is gone, the results are unalterable. But we just cannot seem to turn loose. It is the aging athlete still playing past prime, to the embarrassment of his/her fans. It is the senior manager not accepting when it is time to go and give the job over to others. It is the regular social gathering or civic group whose purpose and services have been outlived. It is the personal dreams and ambitions that refuse to die. We are increasingly haunted by that past moment. We avoid new experiences fearing that that past experience and outcome will reappear in our future. What we should be doing today, what we should be working towards for tomorrow, gets crowded out by these thoughts reaching back to the past. We do not move forward, get on with the current, experience the things that still await us. Our life becomes a rerun.

In attachment, we are not just linked to our past, a product of our past, a wiser person for the lessons learned by our past experiences. Instead, we *live* in the past, like a phonograph needle or a CD reader stuck in a groove, unable to move to the next track. A car tire spinning in the snow, going nowhere, being stuck made even worse as we increase the pressure on the accelerator. Our happiness can be nurtured by a healthy appreciation of what we have done, what we have survived. Unhappiness is inevitable when we attempt to make our present (and our future) a resurrected past. What is done is done. What is past is past.

> "If you have fear of some pain or suffering,
> you should examine whether there is
> anything you can do about it.

> If you can, there is no need to worry about it.
> If you cannot do anything,
> then there is also no reason to worry."
> (H.H. Dalai Lama)

Seeking Perfection, Faulting Others
Under this heading, the Attachment is to <u>Unrealistic Expectations</u>. Life is not perfect. At least not in the way we may wish it to be perfect. We believe that good experiences do not last; bad experiences last too long. Dreams do not succeed; people do not cooperate with our ambitions. Intellectually we have learned that perfection is rarely accomplishable. But emotionally we continue to seek it, expect it, in our lives. And when those expectations are not met, the strength of our attachment can dictate the depth of our disappointment and our negative response.

We expect people to do what they said they would do for or with us, even though we know they have complicated lives of their own. We expect people to fulfill our projected image of perfection that we demand of them – the perfect spouse, the perfect child, the perfect boss – even though our expectations blind us from seeing the truth of who that person truly is. We expect other people to do things exactly as we would do them, even though we would never agree to the reverse commitment. We expect a meal cooked by others to be perfectly done to our taste expectations, even though we insist on making meals for those others the way we choose to cook. We expect things to be built, repaired, operated or provided to us exactly as we expect them to be done. Yet we bristle when others may ask the same reciprocity of us.

When our expectation of perfection is not achieved, it typically morphs into a state of ongoing criticism. We begin to see things as "the glass half empty" cliché. Placing blame is a constant exercise; who is at fault is quickly designated and announced, rather than just accepting or sharing the imperfection and moving on. A sense of proportion is lost: all imperfections are duly noted with blame assigned regardless of the level of real importance of any given situation. Little miscues easily become molehills which become mountains which become interpersonal tsunamis of crisis. In truth, it is not the imperfection itself that is the focus of our attention. It is the Grand Drama that unfolds around the occurrence. Perspective is lost; fixing the problem – if it really is a problem, or one that actually needs fixing – is secondary to the Great Story unfolding.

Characteristically, over time and repetition this attachment leads to a person who continually sees the negative in life, because that negative view has supposedly been reinforced by the many shortcomings of a person's experience – or his interpretations of his experiences. Nothing is ever quite right. What is wrong is usually the first observation made, not what is right. Deserving statements of appreciation get lost in the immediacy of the criticism. Blame is mandatory to establish right away; keeping score is important.

Most of the time these traits are pushed outward to other people, to the things those people do or create. But in some instances, these traits can turn inward. We see ourselves as the imperfection: nothing we do is ever good enough, and it is I who is to blame. It perhaps gets to the point that we even give up trying in the first place because it is all futile. We avoid putting ourselves into a competitive setting where we will be judged (or scored) and found wanting, because we can already presume the negative outcome. It becomes a fatalistic view of "why bother?"

The attachment of Unrealistic Expectations comes when we realize that we have defined perfection as "how I expect it to be, how I expect it to be done." We act from a presumption that a "perfect" thing is an absolute, a commonly shared definition. Yet in reality perfection is a *relative* perspective, truly defined "in the eyes of the beholder." And when others prove to not share our version of perfection, or refuse to accept the mantle of blame being forced their way, personal conflicts inevitably ensue. Being attached to perfection invites unhappiness in ourselves and turmoil for others, because the perfection we seek is so inherently elusive. Expanding our range of acceptability is a necessary step to achieving happiness with our surroundings and what is offered to us.

> "Perfection is not attainable.
> But if we choose perfection we can catch excellence."
> (Vince Lombardi, NFL coach)

A Story – "It Must Be Perfect"
I once had the responsibility of managing a very talented computer programmer. She was technically very competent, with a good sense for design creativity. The problem with her, for her, was the emotional toll it typically took to complete her assigned projects. Because for her, every project became a new pursuit for "perfection," and a battle against the demons of imperfection.

When a project assignment came to her, she would consider how her skills could create the ultimate computer solution, the grandest scheme, the most visually-pleasing screen graphics, the greatest number of tests and functions accomplishable. While the expansiveness might seem magnificent in the abstract, it would often ignore the many practical realities and necessities of real-world constraints that affect every project. For example, constraints about available funding for the budget; short timelines to deliver a finished result; other projects competing for time and attention; the client's ability to take on responsibility for contributing to a large project; the client's need for an elegant solution, versus putting in place a simple and easily manageable solution for the client's employees.

In the eyes of this programmer, all of these "practical" considerations were nothing but obstacles to creating the perfection of "what could be." So the project inevitably would become one battle after another. She would be angry about supposedly being left out of business discussions and resulting decisions; she would be resentful at her supervisors for their failure to support her; she would be frustrated by the client's inability to see the "obvious benefits" of what she would be proposing – often forgetting that technology, and her software group, existed not to advance technology for its own sake but to *create solutions for a client's needs*. And sometimes a client's needs were very simple – to just get the necessary work done for which his/her office was accountable.

In the end, her projects were always completed. On time. Within the assigned budget. And the client would be satisfied with the final product. But oftentimes completion would hold off until the last possible moment, as if the longer she held onto the assignment the longer the professional judgment of her would be deferred. Personal relationships would inevitably be frayed, the wounds a little deeper after each episode. For this programmer, positive end results would be overlooked, there would be minimal satisfaction about her performance, and her emotional strengths would be drained. Perfection was not an inspiring aspiration to the doing of good work. It was the minimal requirement that drove her work, and thereby undermined her ability to see the real contribution she could make. In her eyes, it was always "they" that were at fault for this imperfect product. "They" had forced imperfection onto her, and such imperfection was her own personal failure. She never understood that she, and her insistence on and her attachment to perfection, were the common links in all of these repeated episodes. It was a failure of perspective and understanding that she would take with her to each assignment, to each boss, to each job, and to each employer in her continuing search for "the perfect job." In truth, the imperfection was not in "they"; it was always within her in her attachment to perfection.

Running From What Scares Us
Under this heading, the Attachment is to <u>Our Fears</u>. Fear is one of our most fundamental and powerful emotions. It underlies and stimulates most of our other "negative" emotions. Taken to the extreme, it can lead to various forms of phobias, paranoia or psychosis that can paralyze one's life. In such cases, a full mental health treatment is mandated, treatment well beyond the scope of this book and any spiritual or self-awareness program.

But in less dire circumstances, we can still be significantly constrained by an attachment to our fears. We can develop all kinds of thought processes, personality traits, and actions taken that are primarily driven by a need to hide or disguise our fears. The "objects" of our attachment are not really the many habits of thoughts, views, speech or actions that we develop, but the fear itself. Seeing and acknowledging that fear(s) is of primary importance.

A commonly held attachment is a fear of failure. Failure of whatever type of endeavor. We live in a highly judgmental society, with a high premium placed on success and a large rebuke for failure. Even though we often learn and grow far more from our failures than our successes. What creates a successful entrepreneur, inventor, artist, explorer, etc. is either their absence of concern about failure – they know they will land on their feet, recover, and live another day – or their ability to transcend that fear and use it to drive them to greater efforts and resulting higher outcomes. Conversely, when we attach too much importance to fearing failure, it leads to never even trying. Our fear leads to doubt leads to fatalism leads to the very failure we fear. Our fear drives us into justifying our original fear. Hence the person who continually "screws up and fails" – even though there is likely great competency held dormant underneath the weight of the attachment to failure.

> "I have constructed 3,000 different theories
> in connection with the electric light …
> Yet only in two cases did my experiments
> prove the truth of my theory."
> (Thomas Edison)

Similarly, we may fear whether we are truly qualified and worthy of our exterior successes. We do not feel genuinely competent for our promotion, for our new job, for our new responsibility, for our new recognition. We live in fear of the "pink slip" coming or our customers no longer finding our door. "Circumstances and luck" have conspired to put us where we find ourselves, and we live in fear of our incompetency and un-qualifications being discovered. This was a phenomenon observed in career women in the 1980s/1990s who were making the first inroads into corporate executive roles. Regardless of their experience and certifications, many such women lived in doubt, dreading that the real truth would come out through their anticipated failure. Some fear of such exposure continues to this day.

Similar to being attached to a fear of "being exposed" is a fear of "being caught." We live with high expectations of ourselves to always do the right thing, to always be "good." So on those occasions when we naturally fall short (because we are human!), we try to deny or hide our "failure" – from others, and perhaps from ourselves. But by so doing, we then live in fear of being caught in our denial, our lie, our guilt. It can leave us continually looking over our shoulder, suspicious of others, a general tendency to cloak our self in mystery and withdrawal. We may appear on surface as just "one of the quiet ones," but in fact in attachment we are shunning attention so as to "not be caught," trying to simply fade into the woodwork. It makes for a very tense, self-defensive life that avoids full participation and interaction with others.

Fear inherently leads to a lack of confidence in our future. That lack of confidence can cause us to worry incessantly about how future events will turn out, and to focus on the many (imagined) impediments that could cause plans to go wrong. This form of attachment can lead to a propensity to over-plan, worrying about each and every little detail. We have difficulty being able to just "wing it," a discomfort in leaving some specifics to be worked out as we go. We do not have confidence in our ability to handle the unknown, so we try to make that unknown as knowable as possible in advance in our mind's imagination. In this environment, we may be excellent, and very valuable to a group, in getting the early basic shape of a plan pulled together. We are very organized, but it can be difficult to know when to stop planning, when to leave some details to be dealt with if/when they are encountered. Lacking confidence in our ability to solve problems on the fly, not being able to discriminate what we really need to know when, our planning never knows when to stop. This continuing drive for details and answers can morph our organizing strengths into a pettiness over excruciating details, delay our moving forward with any plan, thereby exhausting friends and family and creating much tension and unhappiness in our relationships.

> "Plans are useless, but planning is invaluable."
> (Winston Churchill)

We may choose to live in fear of many of Life's events and circumstances, typically focusing on health, safety, crime, transportation accidents, etc. These things represent threats to our well-being, and can take us beyond reasonable, prudent precaution into extraordinary avoidance. We avoid travel, live behind locked doors, worry about tainted cuisine, build our days around visits to doctors. Our story becomes one of what lurks around the corner, what tragedies await us, how dangerous life constantly is. Our view of life ignores statistical projections – the odds of one person being in an airline crash, becoming a victim of a crime, falling sick with a particular devastating illness – because our only perspective is that that one statistical person could be <u>me</u>.

> "I've had many problems in my life,
> most of which have never happened."
> (Mark Twain)

The attachment is to fear, the reaction is an avoidance of opportunities and experiences, and the objects selected for expressing our attachment are unlimited. Yet as we "avoid" as a strategy for self-protection, deep inside we know we have made a choice between two options. We know that there is much we are missing out on as we hide in the shadows of our fears, rather than basking in the sunlight of living. We feel a gnawing unhappiness from a life deprived, incomplete, with potential not fully realized. Happiness accepts the realities of our ups and downs, and accepts them as partial payments for living an enriched, full life.

> "Far better it is to dare mighty things,
> to win glorious triumphs,
> even tho checkered by failure,
> than to take rank with those poor spirits
> who neither enjoy much nor suffer much,
> because they live in the gray twilight
> that knows not victory nor defeat."
> (Theodore Roosevelt)

Lights, Camera, Action

Under this heading, the Attachment is to <u>Drama</u>. We are all moved by good narratives of literature, by a well-written stage play, by an engaging movie script. These creative works can bring attention and focus to a character's life, tell a unique story with that character as the centerpiece, create an empathetic audience for the character's sufferings, illustrate courage in the face of overwhelming difficulty, and generate inspirational applause for the character's notable achievements and virtue. A good drama can propel a seemingly mundane, everyday life into a rarified purpose for being.

An occasional dose of drama in one's life can unfold in a perfectly acceptable manner. Everyone has experiences that have dramatic elements that may weigh heavily on us or even be life-changing. But over time we properly work through these periodic episodes and return to the needed balance in our life that sustains us. Yet sometimes these moments of drama can feel very special to us, a moment where we seemed to be the very center of our universe, and that taste of drama can feel quite intoxicating. When that happens, we can become attached not to the real story of our life, but to experiencing the extra drama that we can create around our life.

When we feel that the work that we do, the life that we live, the aspirations that we have, are not adequate in and of themselves, the temptation to enhance "our story" slips into our thinking and our conduct. The feeling of inadequacy may come from a belief that we suffered from a lack of attention, being ignored, or being treated as unimportant. In response, we attach ourselves not to the circumstances of our life, but to the dramas that we can envelop them within. We become the "script doctor" for our self-narrative. And so we add elements of crisis, of severity, of immediacy, of danger to our otherwise everyday circumstances. Bouts of illness become visits to the hospital emergency room; a project becomes potentially career-breaking; a work timeline is backed up to the last minute, completion always in doubt; a task is made extensively complex, with endless critical steps-after-step required to get done; a change in our circumstances becomes a life-threatening event.

It is not the individual instances of drama that illustrate our attachment to drama. Each such individual event can be a quite reasonable level of drama on its face. It is in the *pattern of frequent repetition* of the drama that our attachment takes hold. Over time, our audience becomes worn out from our constant movement from one dramatic episode to the next; the frequency with which "normal life events" become "major dramatic episodes" looks increasingly suspicious. So that audience begins to pull back, unable and/or unwilling to continue to be drawn into these dramatic productions.

Because that is what happens with our attachment to drama. It is not enough to create the drama for ourselves. We must necessarily draw other actors into our play. Suffering in silence does not fulfill our attachment. Others must be brought in to support our plot; "rescue us" from impending physical or mental disaster; affirm the depth of our story and the uniqueness of our circumstance. ("No one else has possibly experienced this suffering I am experiencing.") These supporting players may perform their role for a while – witness a parent's unending engagement with their problematic adult child. But over time, these supporting players grow weary of the constant turmoil, recognize their inability to make a lasting difference, and begin to pull away and set limits on their personal involvement. They have their own lives to live, hopefully unattached to their own dramas. As they progressively pull away, we are unable to hear their concerns, their alternative perspectives, about our drama. We are too invested in holding onto and telling our story, versus listening to their critical reviews. They are there only to continually reaffirm our story, not to alter it. They are only the actors, not the co-authors. So we let them go and seek out new supporting actors for our play. The scope of our drama continues to increase in order to better entice the new actors we are bringing on to the scene.

Drama is intoxicating. It is addictive. It can also become self-destructive. The more drama we bring into our life, the increasing level of drama is needed to sustain it. We attach ourselves to this dramatic ride, and like the thrill-seeker, the drama must constantly expand, always seek "more." Our dramas can be comforting to us, justifying to us. But attaching ourselves to such perpetual script writing is never a way to happiness. Happiness only comes by being comfortable with, and accepting of, the life we actually have. Nothing extra is required. The drama of our ordinary life is drama enough. "Our ordinary life" already within us is where our happiness can be found.

> "If you had a sad childhood, so what?
> You can dance with only one leg
> and see the snowflake falling with only one eye."
> (Robert Bly, poet)

ATTACHMENT TO PERCEPTIONS OF SELF

Negativism and Intolerance
Under this heading, the Attachment is to <u>Fear of the New</u>. The one constant in all of life is Change. What we were a minute ago is not who we are now. We were born; we will die; no negotiation. Every passing second is a new thought, a new experience, a new cell in our body, a new mark on our calendar. The human world is so vast in its scope, and our relative timetable is so short, it is impossible to fully experience, comprehend, or master the life we have. For some, embracing that journey of experience is the exciting reason for life itself. For others, the journey is too daunting, beyond our capability, continually filled with danger just around the corner. Hence Change is a trip to be avoided and defended against constantly. Fear is the underlying watchword, however cleverly masked.

When our training feels limited, our skill set insufficient, our track record questionable, our confidence low, we will usually take the avoidance route. We find a set of circumstances for our life that feels comfortable – career, family structure, political views, religious beliefs, financial position, community – and we wrap ourselves into that comfortable blanket and refuse to come out. We become "set in our ways": the mealtime plate is an exercise in repetitive habit; the TV schedule is lined up with familiar shows; the same route to work is followed to get to the same job – routine is the dominant driver. Failure lurks behind most doors: we do not start new explorations; new ventures are presumed to fail; risks usually outweigh opportunities; vacations emphasize familiar sights and territory.

Bigotry arises: contrasting ideas against our thinking are just plain "wrong"; alternative lifestyles are immoral or impractical; other cultures are "not like us"; strangers are not to be trusted; "those people" are scary – they should become like me, rather than me having to embrace them; they are inherently lesser than I; they are out to harm me, change me.

Attachment to Fear of the New is a life lived "on hold." New learning stops; the neighborhood shrinks; the people in our community look the same – just like me.

Assessing future risks, planning for contingent issues, and moving cautiously can be a very effective way to navigate our lives – as long as we are moving forward. But in attachment, "tomorrow" is all about what can go wrong, a disaster lying in wait to happen. We do not know if we can handle that disaster, and given our concerns, we likely cannot. Safety is in what we already know, have already done, in proven results already in hand; reducing the odds of danger and failure by *eliminating* risk, rather than by trying to *manage* risks. It is a life lived in a very small bowl that sits in an extensive china cabinet; so many other possibilities are available to be tasted. Not every dish can be taken out and used, certainly, but a good number of them can be with wonderful results. As we sit in that one solitary dish, the world is moving on around us, passing us by, leaving us behind. And therein lies our unhappiness. Being attached to our fear of life, we fail to live our life.

> "Change is great. You go first."
> (Saying on a T-shirt)

Defensive Strategies
Under this heading, the Attachment is to <u>Controlling Life</u>. It is a strategy for defending ourselves against our fears of what could go wrong, how we could be hurt. We take on the enormous (and impossible) task of taking that which surrounds us that we do not like, and trying to remold it into a changed form that would then be acceptable to us. It is a way of selecting out from Life only those

things that we like to fill our space. It is a way to prevent what we do not like from entering our space.

Unfortunately, in this one-sided selected fantasy world we have attempted to create, true reality keeps knocking on our door. The first line of our defense is simply to not hear the knocking, to not see who/what stands on the other side. Being blind and tone-deaf can work for us for a while – until something significant and powerful enough happens to burst through our protective isolation and demand our attention. At which point defeating the beast that threatens our illusion and our sense of well-being becomes Objective #1. The battle – to control or to be controlled – begins its life or death struggle.

The attachment of Control can take many forms, and is very closely connected to the Fear of the New attachment. But whereas the Fear of the New typically results in a passive, "hold to the status quo" posture, the Control strategy is a very aggressive and visible pattern. Control usually evolves from a very personal, multi-linked thought process that, in its present form, can be very hard for us to easily see in ourselves and understand. The Control reflex can arise only periodically from occasional triggers, or it can come to dominate our life.

The typical labels people use to describe those with control attachments are "bossy," "critical," and "control freak." Control people frequently interfere and offer unsolicited advice or opinions, and they also <u>expect</u> their advice to be taken – even though the listener may not have ever asked for such advice. There is only one way that tasks should be done, meals should be cooked, cars should be driven – i.e. "my way." The way other people might choose to do something is not just an alternative method, a different version; it is simply "wrong." Which leads to frequent criticism of others, and words to correct them about how things should be done. Things done wrong are the first focus of conversation; things done right go without mentioning. The

Control person uses criticism to cut down to size a more powerful or accomplished individual; having been diminished by such criticism, the once powerful can now be met on a more equal footing.

Our need for control often results in our rejecting assistance being offered from others. We find it difficult to ask for help, or if we do, we seek to dictate to our helpers in detail exactly how the task should be done. Out of growing frustration, we may literally take the task (or the tool or implement) out of the helper's hands to do it ourselves. Due to our insistence at doing things ourselves, we often overwork ourselves with effort and/or time; this potentially leads to feelings of martyrdom, and frustration that other people do not adequately see and appreciate all of our (self-inflicted) dedication. Our inability to accept alternative methods for doing a task, or an alternative manner of outcome to be achieved, makes it very difficult to delegate our responsibilities (or some portion thereof) to others. The craving to assert our dominance, and our failure to see the needs of others and support their efforts, makes us poor managers and administrators. We may be great individual performers, but not so great at being leaders of others when teamwork is needed.

The need to control often influences the choices of career. A classroom can be a perfect place to dictate how students will conduct themselves to our standards. A management career can provide a perfect setting for telling others what to do. A physician can have ultimate authority over the life or death of another. A parent can see an empty palate in the child who waits to be instructed by us about almost everything. A spouse can be shaped into exactly the partner we have been expecting all along. After all, we are (supposedly) doing these things "for their own good."

It can all seemingly go fine – for a while. Until the object of our controlling attachment begins to kick back. They rebuff the unwelcome advice, or decide to follow a different course after all.

Or they continue to do it "wrong" anyway: a door to "passive aggression" begins to open. Or the controlee begins to drift away and put space in between the controller – perhaps slowly at first, then more distance gained more quickly. A different catch-22 may begin: as the controlee pulls away, the controller pushes harder to bring things back into line, the controlee pulls even further away, the controller pushes even harder; a vicious cycle emerges. It continues unstoppable until a complete break occurs: the controlee either shuts down and goes emotionally numb but stays in the relationship; or the controlee walks away, likely never to return. The spouse walks out; the employee quits for a new job; the infant cries and screams irrationally; the grown child moves across country; the invitations from friends no longer come.

The same attempt at "control but a resulting loss of control" can also be experienced with inanimate or "institutional" objects. In the mind of the Control person, the car "intentionally" broke down in the middle of our long-awaited vacation. The weather refused to cooperate with our necessary outdoor projects. The caterer canceled our dinner party at the last minute. The doctor's patients died on him in spite of his heroic effort and great skills and the scope of their disease. Our church does not provide a "proper" religious service. Our civic club does not do things the way we think they should be done. Government does not do the things we think it should; or, conversely, government tries to interfere and boss us around too much. Other nations and their governments refuse to follow our country's lead. No one seems to cooperate with our good insight and expectations. We somehow forget that institutions are simply a collected and semi-organized mass of people, and these institutions will reflect the same characteristics – including emotional attachments – that exist individually in their key people.

> "Everything that irritates us about others
> can lead us to an understanding about ourselves."
> (Carl Jung)

When our craving for control is thwarted, our reaction is likely a very difficult and jarring emotional response. Our solid defense line – control – has been broken. We may react verbally – fierce arguments ensue, a sharp tongue lashes out. We may react physically – we retreat to the bed with a migraine headache, or perhaps even dangerous violence is exchanged. Our personality becomes consistently disagreeable, grumpy, short-tempered, angry. Thwarted control is not a pretty sight.

We think that, with control, we can selectively pick, choose and mold the happiness we wish to draw into our lives. But it is an assumption destined to fail because of its false premise: that we can permanently control much of anything besides ourselves. (And even our control of self can be quite limited.) We can influence others; we can facilitate change in our surroundings if others agree to the change. The President of the United States is said to be the most powerful individual in the world, yet most ex-Presidents say that they spent most of their presidency *reacting* to people and unanticipated events that they could not control.

Control, if any at all, is only a temporary exercise at best, and is rarely genuine. It is a pretend life. When we try to use control in order to gain our happiness, we virtually guarantee our unhappiness from that which cannot be controlled.

> "When you think you *deserve, expect,* or *need* something specific to happen, you are setting yourself up for constant unhappiness and a final inability to enjoy or at least allow what is actually going to happen … Practice giving up control early in life. You will be much happier and much closer to the truth, to the moment, and to God – none of which can be experienced when you presume you can be in control anyway."
> (Fr. Richard Rohr)

<u>*Seeking Honors and Approbations*</u>
Under this heading, the Attachment is to <u>External Approbations</u>. When we feel that we are a lesser person – not as smart, not as attractive, not as talented, not as successful, not as … – one of the most powerful antidotes to that feeling is someone else speaking words of praise to us. The positive words of others carry far more weight to us than our own words to ourselves. But if the praise and acknowledgment come in through the door of attachment, then they are like raindrops devoured by a barren desert, dewdrops lost into a bottomless well. The craving is far too great for them to make any permanent difference in the landscape.

In attachment we strive for recognition over and above the quality of our performance itself. Without the recognition, the effort and quality of our work seem somewhat unsatisfying, incomplete. Our own self-compliments feel inadequate to our need for confirmation. We become adept at figuring out what brings praise, and then we mold our lives toward that which will bring the needed attention. Our craving for praise trumps our real goal to follow our own true Life path.

So we work long and extra hours, sacrificing friends and family relationships, because that is where the bonus paycheck lies. We volunteer for extra assignments because that is where the promotion comes from. We study extra hours in test preparation because that is where the scholarship comes from. We practice endlessly shooting hoops because that is where the sports contract is signed. We pursue our acting or musical performance ambitions because that is where the applause is heard. All of that hard work improves our skills and accomplishments. But it is the thrill, and the pursuit of the thrill, that transcend the work itself. Yet the glory is only for a moment; the work demands continue on; the pursuit of recognition is endless.

It is under External Approbations where "winning" also comes in. The Objective of a contest may be to "win" over an opponent, defined as scoring more points, having more chips, accumulating more money, getting to the finish line first, garnering more votes, raising more donations, selling more inventory, rationalizing better points in a debate. But the real Purpose of a contest is to challenge ourselves, measure our standing, have fun, and experience the joy of achieving a goal. When the Purpose gets lost and we become attached only to the Objective (i.e. winning), then trouble follows. The fighter seeks not to outbox, but to violently pummel his opponent into submission. For the athlete, "taking out" an opponent by injury becomes the chosen tactic over finessing by superior skills. For the businessperson, lines of unethical behavior are crossed to obtain riches by deception or callous double-dealing, if not outright criminal actions. For the politician, principles are given away by taking any position, saying whatever is necessary, just to win the election. Yet all of these victories are short-lived because the recognition ends quickly, the next contest appears, and new replacement challengers are always in the wings waiting for their turn to knock us off our pedestal.

A related trait to the attachment to External Approbations is false modesty. When words of praise are received in attachment, the compliment is rebuffed by saying such things as, "Oh, I wasn't really that good," or "I don't really deserve this." Sometimes this may be a frank (though unintended or unconscious) admission of our actual belief in our adequacy. Or we think that such demurring comments demonstrate commendable humility. But it is a disingenuous humility that actually seeks to elicit even more recognition of us: our rebuff essentially demands a repeat statement of the compliment, and the package now includes the additional recognition of our supposed modesty.

Or, in lieu of feigned humility, arrogance sets in and bragging becomes the resulting response. We do not risk waiting for the compliments of others. We jump right in and supply the recognition ourselves, write our own script. We control the dialog about ourselves before anyone else has a chance to; we then are able to say exactly what we want to hear. And we make a point of letting everyone know just how talented and accomplished we are.

> "... a senior astronaut got on [a crowded elevator] and just stood there, visibly impatient, waiting for someone to divine that he needed to go to the 6th floor, and push the button. 'I didn't spend all those years in university to wind up pushing buttons in an elevator,' he snapped ... For me, it was a cautionary tale about the pitfalls of ever thinking of yourself as An Astronaut (or A Doctor, or A Whatever). To everyone else, you are just that arrogant guy on the elevator, craving significance ... This might seem self-evident, but it can't be, because so many people do it."
> (Col. Chris Hadfield, astronaut)

When a compliment is received without attachment, the kindness is genuinely appreciated, acknowledged to the giver with a simple "thank you," and then let go. No change either way is made in the person's sense of herself; "her head is not turned," as the saying goes. There is no need to rub salt into the wound or nose into the mud of an opponent's defeat.

Without attachment, one is able to step in and do the work quietly, see it to completion, and then step back, unconcerned with who gets the credit. Good coaches and managers know that performers who are focused on recognition rather than the game itself make lousy team players who do not play well with others, no matter how great their individual skills may be. The constant craving to be "the star" diminishes the odds of achieving a group victory; the dissention raised if the singular attention does not come creates distraction for everyone involved. It is best to put such people into solo competitions or standalone tasks that are not interdependent with others.

Great competitors and contributors are a joy to behold. The work they put in to be capable of such superior performance is to be admired and commended. But when they lose their perspective on the work versus the approval of it, they can become a disturbing presence to be around. One win is never enough; one award is insufficient; the next challenge always awaits; losing is an intolerable temper-tantrum; a gracious loser cannot be found in this person; the insatiable thirst for recognition never ceases. It is not by coincidence that so many who are attached to Public Approbation (versus the work itself) self-destruct so often, and so prematurely. When we are attached to External Approbations we never really enjoy the win, cannot accept and appreciate the praise. Because it never really fills the hole deep in our heart. The praise we get becomes a narcotic for the praise we have yet to get. And on it goes. The momentary happiness of recognition fades into the unhappiness of constantly seeking out the next reward.

> "This is the way of heaven:
> do your work, then quietly step back."
> (Lao-Tzu, "Tao te Ching")

Riding The White Horse

Under this heading, the Attachment is to <u>Saving the World</u>. As a religious person living within a religious culture, we are encouraged to right wrongs, to seek justice for all, and to help out our neighbors in their times of sorrow or desperation. It is an appeal not just to our nobler self, but also a call to take *action* from that nobler self. So we embark on such greater missions, and justifiably feel deep satisfaction from such endeavors.

Left unchecked, however, our nobility of purpose can lead us into very personal trouble and dangerous circumstances. We attach ourselves to the self-perception of "the Savior" who will rise and save the day for all. But in so doing, we often lose the judgment to properly choose which battles to fight; where we can be most effective with our time and abilities; which battles to pass and let go by. We typically see ourselves as the *only* person qualified or available to do battle, thusly elbowing out opportunities for others to get involved in The Just Cause. We may not listen to the good advice of others in how the battle should be fought, the Cause advanced; we rush in foolishly and stumble in our efforts, and take our defeats as very personal failures. Unfortunately, we may also discover that we have spent so much time pursuing the Noble Crusade, and invested so much energy in our efforts, that we have no time or energy left over for our daily responsibilities or for the loved ones we hold dear – loved ones we have left on the sidelines of our life.

There is also a co-rider that frequently shares the white horse with us. That co-rider is Passion. A certain amount of passion is helpful in steeling us for the noble battles we fight. It is a reservoir we can draw from when our resolve and courage begins to be exhausted. Passion can be that extra shot of oxygen we need as other fall to the sidelines gasping for a breather. But if our passion is mined from the same mountain as our attachment, then it will simply further stoke the fire that is already consuming us. Our mis-directions, our deafness to advice, our stumbles, and our self-importance will all be pushed to even higher levels of self-expectation. The fuel of righteousness is replaced by the self-immolation fire of anger: an unquenchable anger that runs roughshod over the concerns, ideas, and legitimate considerations of others – the very others we often need to be successful in our Cause. That kind of insatiable passion is not a reservoir to drink from; it is a tidal wave that overwhelms and absorbs us.

> "Why do you want this for us
> more than we want it for ourselves?"
> (Sharon Shevlin, college administrator)

The world needs "doers" who give of themselves to achieve larger goals. Who will "fight the good fight" that others are willing to let pass by. But when we overly attach ourselves to <u>our role</u> (and our self-importance) in that Cause, the Cause itself is diminished. This attachment often comes from our own perception of a weakness experienced at some point in our life. That moment(s) when we felt powerless to protect or advance our own being. When that long-suffering hole in our being asserts itself, we then attach ourselves to external battles that we believe we can now fight successfully. The Cause(s) we take up becomes a proxy fight for the old battle in which we were unable to engage and win. And so our current involvement is not truly focused on the Cause itself; it is focused on our own personal stake in the fight. As part of our attachment, when we win it is also important to us for everyone to know who was riding atop that white horse leading the charge. The cheers of the saved are the needed fuel that feeds our ride.

In this battle derived from a base of attachment, any satisfaction gained from temporary victories will be short-lived. The happiness of the moment will soon be replaced by that more fundamental unhappiness deep inside of us that knows that the next battle to be fought awaits us, and the next after that, and so on endlessly. Because the original battle was lost, these proxy battles will also lose in the long run. It is only by recognizing our true motivation for our ride on the white horse, and then calling on our humility to truly subjugate ourselves to the Noble Cause – just one player among many contributing what we can – that we will find true happiness in our worthwhile efforts to better the world.

> "The way to get things done
> is not to mind who gets the credit."
> (Benjamin Jowett, 19th-century English clergyman)

<u>Living To Satisfy Others</u>
Under this heading, the Attachment is to <u>Outside Expectations of You</u>. In this attachment, our own identity, our own ambitions, our own desires, our own pursuits, our own definitions of success, are dismissed and replaced by what others tell us that they expect of us. In our desire to please them, to not fail them, their expectations of us become our expectations of ourselves. And we gear our life expecting to succeed fully in those expectations.

Generally, little of this is done deviously or surreptitiously. It is all above board, verbalized openly without subtlety. An expectation becomes presumed, a given. The expectations can be laid upon us at a very early age; sometimes even while still in the womb, others are laying out our life for us, often in exhaustive detail. The script has already been written for us before the casting call is even issued.

These expectations may come from many sources. They are often family-based. The very name we are given may imply expectations that our life will follow a similar path as our namesake (especially with boys named Jr., etc.). A son or daughter may be expected to attend "the right school" that the parents attended, or some other prestigious college. The expectation of following into the family business or profession is often present; acceptable and unacceptable careers may be made clear early on. The expectation of being a caregiver to an aged parent is frequently held over the child's head. The expectation "not to embarrass the family name" can transcend substantive concerns about what actions or lifestyle we may seek to pursue.

Ethnic or religious cultures can create expectations of us. The Jewish ambition of becoming a doctor (or the second choice – a lawyer) is not entirely an ill-founded cliché. Customs dictating inheritance, preferences of gender, role and conduct based upon gender or family position, also serve to create expectations of us.

Cultural definitions of what it means to be "a real man/woman" constantly frames our thinking. And cultural thinking is multi-tiered: what it means, and is expected of us, in being a Texan, a Southerner, an American often precludes life conclusions we might have come to on our own.

Implicit in these expectations of form is an attached expectation of success. Phrases such as "great things are expected of you," or "I look forward to saying 'I knew you when'," or "I'm sure you will succeed better than your [father, mother, sibling, etc.]," all create another level of expectation of "success" for us.

The collective force of these kinds of expectations of us can be a great underlying determinant in how we may think we "choose" to live our lives. If we can take them as suggestions, as guidance, they can help move us to good accomplishments. But if we attach ourselves strongly to these expectations, build our life choices around them and never question whether they are what *we* really want for ourselves, then constant unhappiness will be our likely outcome. Because there will always be one more expectation, one higher rung of success, expected of us. Expected by others; expected of ourselves. It is in this attachment to external expectations that we lose control over our own definition of ourselves. Yet it is only in making our own choices of our own expectations for ourselves that happiness can truly thrive.

Adopting Roles
Under this heading, the Attachment is to <u>False Identity</u>. This attachment has the most boxes filled in our attachment warehouse.

We all wear many different "hats" in our lives. A variety of relationships, responsibilities, and formalized activities. These are the "roles" we are required to play. And each of these roles carries its own label or official title; each title then requires a script to be followed. Like an actor on the stage, we arrive at the theater of our life, step into the role we have been assigned, and act out the scripted part. Except that we often feel like a one-person ensemble company performing all the lead roles in each Act and Scene, with some supporting characters showing up every now and then to help with the performance load. Spread that thin, it is near-impossible to know all of the lines, all of the stage movements, ahead of time. So we look outside of ourselves for some scriptwriters and directors to learn from.

When we are unclear about whom we are, we may explore many roles searching for the right fit for us. If we lack confidence in the dialog, the stagecraft, the right script for a particular role, we pick out and attach ourselves to individuals who appear to be good examples of how that role should be performed. Those individuals may be historical figures we read about and are inspired by (for example, the generations who grew up nurtured on the Horatio Alger poor-boy-to-success story, or Washington's refusal to tell a lie). They may be current people we observe but at a distance, unable to have direct contact. Or they may be part of our current network of people: family, friends, coworkers, professional relationships. So we may learn from a distance; we may learn from direct instructions. However the guidance comes, these teachers become our role models.

If the teacher or mentor is knowledgeable in the topic, skilled in sharing expertise with others, with broad perspective and genuine self-awareness, they can provide a very valuable service to our personal growth. If they are only minimally qualified, with minimal skills in guiding others, come from a narrow perspective of experience, and are rife with their own self-confidence issues, these guides can do real damage to us. The onus is therefore on us to discern the real qualifications of our guides, and to select only those who will serve us well at varying stages of our lives.

Identifying role models to help get us through life can be a perfectly good survival and growth mechanism when we are fairly clear about our direction. But if our sense of self is weak, or our direction is unclear, we are capable of creating and attaching ourselves to roles and role models that will take us far away from our true self. Our desperate search for value and validity leaves us vulnerable to those who would seduce us for their own purposes, vulnerable to losing ourselves entirely in a false role that does not befit us.

So we may take on the noble role of a parent, but perhaps before we are really ready, before our life circumstances can sufficiently support this role, before we have really thought about what it means to be a parent or what kind of parent we intend to be. We just think we want to be "a parent," are *destined* to be a parent, and inherently in our parenthood we will find our happiness.

So also in becoming a spouse, a lover. A son or daughter, a sibling. A grandparent or grandchild. A friend, or even an enemy. An employee, a worker, a coworker, a supervisor, a manager, a vice president, a CEO. A President of the United States. A preacher, a lawyer, a carpenter, a fireman, a forest ranger, a soldier, a stock broker. A civic leader, a charity worker, a hospice volunteer. The chauffer for the children, the family banker, the DIY repairperson, the family cook and/or housecleaner. The list of roles and labels each of us carries is almost endless, in this immediate moment and over our lifetimes, in very obvious roles and very subtle roles.

Sometimes our aspirations and role models are of intangible roles. We focus on a human quality, and select the role models we will emulate based upon who best projects that quality. If "being beautiful" is the role we feel compelled to play, then we will find who we believe to be such a beautiful person and see her in our mirror rather than our self. Witness the high impact over the years of movie stars and fashion houses in signaling what looks are considered glamorous from one day to the next, and how those standards quickly surface in the public so soon thereafter. Or perhaps one selects an honored historical figure that epitomizes "character" or "power," or someone who we feel personifies "compassion" or "the spiritual person." Or someone who truly defines "a true friend." We find that role model we are seeking, learn her life story, memorize his tactics, and then work to reconstruct that other life into our own being in our own different and unique circumstances.

One interesting example on this intangible theme is an attachment to "Freedom." When we have a major concern about potentially being dominated by another (or dominated by life itself), and we fear that we may lack the ability to resist that domination head on, then we may attach ourselves to the necessity of maintaining our sense of personal freedom. In our desperation to be free, the priority is avoiding entangling relationships, commitments to people, or obligation to responsibilities. Nothing to tie us down; nothing to limit our options; always solely the one to make the decisions regarding ourselves. We continually find ways to demonstrate to others how free we are. We are notoriously late for scheduled appointments (calendars are a threat!); we hop from one project to the next – often with much left undone in our wake. Over time, people begin to catch on and ask, who is she trying to convince – us or herself? Our supposed freedom is an illusion. We do not make free choices after all; we *avoid* making choices from fear of loss of self. But we have already lost our self in a cage marked "seeks to be free."

> "Freedom is the ability to make
> both choices and commitment."
> (Jay Leach, UUC minister)

In attachment, we give ourselves to some vision of our role, some individual who we feel personifies that role, some criteria we have constructed to explain that role. We blind ourselves to any negative or destructive elements of that vision, and we entertain little openness to any alternative visions or any criticisms of our model. We give ourselves over fully to the model we have attached to, and give little thought or continuing assessment to the truthfulness of that model or its appropriateness for us. We strongly defend our interpretation of the role, and hold fast to it unless or until some major external failure occurs to us.

The marriage fails, choking under the constrictions of a model that did not truly reflect the individual selves of the marriage partners. The students rebel or fail, raising serious questions about the teacher's abilities. Without seeing it coming, the employee is fired for incompetency, or failure to properly understand the role demanded, or for not being a team player, or for not acting consistent with the style of the company's environment. The preacher did not spiritually connect with the congregation. The stockbroker let greed override prudent stewardship of people's retirement funds. The family cook finally discovers that no one enjoys his mother's old recipes.

In such difficult cases, the model is finally seen to be lacking. We may choose to dig our heels in even further, still committed that our model and our teacher are correct. Or we may simply latch onto another role model and once again graft someone else's life onto our skin. Or we may stop, spend time reaching inside of our self, and discover what <u>we</u> truly think and believe for ourselves. In which case a slow, evolving change in our self-definition begins to occur. A necessary change that may likely be upsetting to those who have come to expect an old model of our self. But this new self-definition at last comes genuinely from within, not from without; genuinely reflects our real self's creative version of the role, not an old or artificial version simply pasted to our soul.

We often observe roleplaying in young children. It is an important tool to help them develop the sense of who they are, who they may become, what their own creativity is, and how to make some sense of all the unknown that is around them. But as we grow older and our personalities mature, such roleplaying is intended to fall away, give way to our confident sense of who we intrinsically are, and defer to our learned skills on how we will manage our greater scope of relationships. When our self-confidence is instead supported by attachment rather than by skill, by painting a mask of someone else's life over our own, genuine happiness will never be found. Happiness comes from being the unique self that we are, and living only our life and not someone else's. To attempt to live the life of another, to think in the mindset of another, to live a definition of what someone else believes our life should be, is certain to live an unfulfilled and unhappy life.

> "Peace is the result of retraining your mind
> to process life as it is,
> rather than as you think it should be."
> (Wayne Dyer)

<u>A Story</u> – "<u>Giving Away Your Life</u>"
My mother was born with an identical twin sister. So identical that the only telltale difference between them was a small birthmark on my mother's leg. But as identical as they were in physical form, they could not have been more different in personality and character. My mother was more ego-centered, more often putting herself first, highly demanding of others, and sharper of tongue. Hence her family nickname of "the Duchess." Her twin, my aunt, was the gentler one, more often thinking of the welfare of others, giving of herself to their needs, softer of tongue. "The sweet one," as described by those who knew her. As teenagers, they were both exuberant, popular, full-of-life girls – typical teenagers is most respects for the 1930s, independent of spirit and self-sufficient due to their family frequently moving around the country. As they approached their 19th birthdays, they were ready to take on adult life.

They arrived together from their current home in California on a visit to spend time with their many relatives in western Arkansas.

Coming home from a double-date to celebrate their birthday, my aunt complained of not feeling well, of having a very dry mouth. Thereafter, she quickly fell into a coma, and within 24 hours she died. The death, and the complete surprise of it, shocked the entire extended family. Her parents (my grandparents) took the train from California to Arkansas for the funeral – a ceremonial ritual that even further embittered my mother over the loss of her sister rather than comforted her.

Over the next months, the reality of the void, and the depth of the loss, settled in. Not just with my mother, but with the entire extended family. My aunt was that well loved. In the climate of that extreme loss, my mother began to change, began to step in to try to fill that unfillable void. She made a conscious, life-altering decision to replace her twin sister by *becoming* her twin sister. She already had the physical appearance; now she would also become the mind, character and personality of her deceased twin. She would completely attach herself to *being* her sister, in order to console and benefit her remaining family.

And so she did. Four months later, under pressure from my grandparents, she married my father. He was 14 years her senior, but an established local accountant who could give her life stability – an especially important consideration in the midst of the Depression years. In so doing, she rejected her "real true love," a high school sweetheart left behind in North Carolina. She stepped into an adult, wifely role at age 19, and left her carefree, girlish youth behind. She now assumed "the giver" role of her deceased twin, no longer to be "the taker" – but her giving always retained a string, an IOU, attached to it. She worked to diminish the sharpness of her tongue and learned all the sweet words to say – but the still-present criticisms simply came out more disguised, more subtle.

My mother surrendered her real self in favor of fully attaching herself to the would-be life of another. It was not about just aspiring or attaching to some <u>aspect</u> of another, it was *completely becoming another*. However noble her intention, that forced giving up of herself would slowly eat away at her for the rest of her life, and create a false life built upon the sacrifice of self she had made. Her growing martyrdom always expected others to appreciate what she had done, to understand what she had given up. But that recognition of her sacrifice was never sufficiently forthcoming for her. As all of her life's disappointments and failures mounted up, a life attached to being another resulted only in incompleteness, bitterness, and unhappiness. The person she truly was disappeared; the person she tried to become never fully arrived. But once attached, she always remained unbreakably attached to that image. It was a continual struggle that ultimately broke her emotionally and physically. She was never able to allow herself the happiness of simply being who she truly was.

<u>The Greatest Attachment</u>
We have looked at a number of different forms in which attachments can be created and manifest themselves in our lives. Yet these are still just examples; a full list of such forms is limited only by our imagination and individual circumstances. Each will appear uniquely to each of us, even as the themes may be common to many. But beyond the attempt at categorizing and listing, there is one attachment that can transcend all others, encapsulate all others. Under this summary heading, the Attachment is to Being Attached to Unhappiness.

Whatever specific individual attachments we may latch onto for ourselves, the craving to be attached to *something*, to almost anything, can become the transcendent attachment. We want to believe that we are attached to something important, some Purpose, in our life. We believe we need the motivational power that attachment gives to us, that propels us forward each day. We feel that the intensity of emotions that attachment can generate within us gives substance to our life, generates our most personal feelings. We are comforted that attachment to things outside of us – which is where most of our attached objects are found – gives us connections within the often cold, hostile, separated environment in which we live. If our attachments, and the objects to which we are attached, are the very substance of our life, we often think – why would we want to give them up?

At this transcendent level, our various individual forms of attachment are simply the components we have elected to create in this moment, in this phase, of our life. They rise, they fall; they come, they go. When we have exhausted where one attachment can take us, or resolved its hold on us, we then simply go on to create the next form needed to serve our need. Which is why we never seem to make much progress in our "pursuit of happiness." In fact, when we are attached to being attached, we are actually *attached to being unhappy*.

We see attachment to unhappiness when we simply refuse to be happy. No matter what "good" comes out of our efforts, we only see the negative side-consequences. We feel guilty about feeling, much less expressing, our happiness, because "we don't deserve it." We just know that a happy moment "will never last." We back away from pursuing dreams because we know "dreams never come true for us." We avoid competitions or challenges because we are "sure to lose." We avoid deep, long-lasting relationships because we know that ultimately "we will be hurt." Every setback is simply confirmation of the reality of our unhappiness, the statement of our destiny. The back cloud of continual disasters and failure is ever-present, always following us and hanging over our heads.

It is as though we wander in a perpetual fog, always seeking, believing that something good is out there for us, but never sure which direction to go to find it. Life, and happiness, seem above all to be a futile pursuit, a gift reserved for others but not for us, a reward for those deemed worthy. And we are not so worthy.

It is only by directly confronting our doubts, our pessimism, that we can begin to counteract this attachment. We need to examine those instances where we felt that our fatalism was confirmed, and then recognize that it was not Life that defeated our happiness, it was we crippling our own efforts. Because in fact we *are* worthy, and there is no inherent reason, no overriding curse, that requires us to be unhappy. We only have to end our denials, open that door, and choose to allow happiness into our life. Once we open this front entranceway to our happiness, all the other doors of our attachments then present themselves to us to choose to open. Open to allow the breath of happiness to circulate throughout our very being.

7. DISTINGUISHING WANTS FROM ATTACHMENTS

> "And when the farmer has got his house,
> he may not be the richer but the poorer for it,
> and it be the house that has got him ...
> for our houses are such unwieldy property that we are
> often imprisoned rather than housed in them."
> (Henry David Thoreau)

There is an inherent problem we face in identifying our needs, our wants, and our objects of attachments (our cravings). We must properly distinguish between attachments to the objects of our cravings, versus simply having appropriate aspirations and responses to Life's circumstances – the things we do to improve ourselves and enjoy the many good things available from living a full life. It is often a subtle but genuine and important distinction, a distinction that relies on our ability to newly see ourselves honestly and objectively.

When we see just some of the examples of the ways we are capable of attaching ourselves to objects, and how significantly those attachments can affect us in our everyday life, we may tend to recoil from a sense of hopelessness. It can seem like everything we do, every decision we make, comes from a base of attachment. Given this defeatism, we may shut down our potential openness to seeing our life in a new way, and ask, "So is it wrong to want things, or want different circumstances, than we now have? Is it wrong to have an ambition to excel? Is it inappropriate to want 'a better life'?"

The answer most definitely is no, it is not wrong to want things, to be successful, to enjoy what Life has to offer. Hence the differences between those fundamental things we "Need" to survive, the nice things we "Want," and our inexhaustible "Cravings" – those distorted Wants we have transformed into supposed Needs through attachment. The difference is in our <u>intention</u>, and in our <u>intensity</u>.

We *need* to eat food to nourish our bodies and keep them strong; we *want* to savor the taste of good cooking; we *crave* to eat everything in sight from fear of starvation. We *need* a car to get us from place to place; we *want* a new car because our current vehicle is too undependable for long trips; we *crave* a new car because our current one is the oldest one in the neighborhood. We *need* a career to support ourselves and our family; we *want* to be a doctor because translating science into life-saving skills fascinates us; we *crave* being a doctor because it generates prestige and fulfills our parents' ambitions for us. Or we *want* to be a carpenter because we love working creatively with our hands; yet we reject carpentry because all our high school friends are going into white-collar professions, and we *crave* the respect and approval of our friends.

Each of us has an expansive capacity to come up with rationalized, positive motivations for each action we take. Therefore rarely does an action itself reveal much of our true character, our real but disguised self. Words and actions can come from too many possible sources to tell us definitive information. So we have to examine our own motivations, those feelings that stir inside of us, our trains of thoughts and our conclusions drawn, if we are to separate out our reasonable wants versus our self-destructive cravings. From those examined and clarified motivations, we must then look to identify those objects we have created in our minds, and our relationships to them – whether want or crave, freedom or attachment, accurate view or distorted projection. The Outcomes we create come from our minds; but our true Intentions live in our hearts. It is that Truth in the Heart that we need to discover, not the stories we tell ourselves in our minds.

"God knows what is in our hearts."
(The Qur'an)

Anger is a good indicator for when we have formed an attachment above our want, because anger comes from a frustrated clinging, a thwarted drive, an unfilled expectation. Restlessness is also a good indicator that attachment is at work. Indecisiveness, daydreaming, strained relationships with others, extended periods of sadness, disappointment or hopelessness can all be indicators that our attachments are taking excessive control over our lives. It is in desperation that "cravings" – attachments – live.

There is also another good method that can help us to distinguish between our wants and our cravings. When we act out of craving rather than simply fulfilling our wants, there will always be a sense of gratification and pleasure immediately thereafter. The very intensity pushing on us will cause us to feel a great short-term relief when that craving has been temporarily satisfied, that pressure has been released. But satisfying a craving is rarely in our overall and longer-term best self-interest. So relatively quickly after our gratification subsides will come a replacement sense of remorse. It will show up as feelings of regret, sadness, maybe even anger at ourselves, guilt about taking this "selfish indulgence," failure at having given in to our lack of self-control. That bowl of ice cream not on our diet will lose its sweet taste; the first payment for that new car will overwhelm our sense of pride standing in our driveway. If we had in fact been acting only out of Want, our sense of satisfaction would be continual, without the nagging glance over the shoulder. We should not beat ourselves up over such "lapses" in our character, in our resolve. There will be many such trip-ups along the way. We just learn from the experience; we see the attachment more clearly; we prioritize to work on it even harder. We will do better next time.

We can often see attachment in others more easily than in ourselves. In individual instances, what we hear them say or watch them do may seem perfectly reasonable. But over time, we begin to hear the same stories, see the same scenarios, repeat themselves over and over. The circumstances change, the people are different, but the themes are all too familiar. We begin to sense that we have heard this song sung before, have watched this play in reruns. That person's attachments begin to present themselves quite clearly. The question becomes, can we see our own attachments just as clearly as others see our attachments in us?

Living without attachments, our life feels to be in balance. Yes, things continue to not always go our way, or move smoothly; we still have our disappointments if not outright failures. Hurtful things happen, losses are experienced. We allow sufficient time for a natural response of sadness or grief in those moments, but we pass through them relatively quickly and do not linger. Unencumbered by distorted objects and false attachments to them, we find a new path to travel, a new aspiration to follow, a new challenge to take on. We do these new things informed by our previous experience, and with a confidence that an appropriate alternative course exists and a different fulfillment awaits us. It is a life that pursues wants, but always knows that many options exist to fulfill those wants. We are free and able to select the options of greatest good for us. It is in such a life, lived in truthful reality without fear or false attachments, that happiness lives.

> "Detachment is not that you should own nothing,
> but that nothing should own you."
> (Ali ibn abi Talib, early Moslem teacher)

8. THE JOURNEY TO UNATTACHED LIVING

If we accept that "mental attachments" exist, that they exist not just in others but also in us, then we are at a crossroad. Will we continue to live as we have been under the yoke of our attachments, pursuing endless dead-end trails? Or, will we begin to cut the bindings of those attachments, empty the many boxes in our vast attachment warehouse, and live a free and more fulfilling life? Will we end the accumulation of more boxes of attachment and instead focus our efforts on allowing ourselves the happiness to which we are entitled?

At first glance, the easier answer might seem to be to cut attachments and live in happiness. In fact, the *easier* answer is to keep doing what we have been doing. To keep on living as we have been. Because our attachments, however destructive or limiting to us, serve as our old familiar friends. We are well-versed in creating them, and well-practiced in living them. It is easier to live in our habits than to change our habits.

The unfortunate truth is that changing our lives is hard work. Seeing our own attachments, seeing the places where they have taken us over the years, seeing the impacts that they have had on our life, and then mustering up the courage and will to change these deeply embedded aspects of us, is very hard and scary work. "Wanting" to live without attachment is easy. Having the -strength and determination to do so requires Commitment in the truest sense. It is a long journey; it requires a significant investment of time; it is a journey filed with obstacles and frustration; it will change not just you but also the people and circumstances around you. It can also be a lonely journey at times, because as you change some "old friends" – people and your circumstances – will not be able to make the journey with you, not willing and able to accept who you are becoming. Because you will no longer serve the needs they have of you for their own attachments.

So the first question is not whether we wish to live the unattached life of our true self and the happiness that comes from that. The real first question is whether we are willing to make the difficult journey required to realize the ease of happiness.

> "You must understand the work that is in front of you
> for your spiritual journey, and know the cost required.
> If you are not prepared to make the level of effort that is required,
> do not set out on a foolhardy mission."
> (Lesson 56, *Lessons From The Teacher Jesus*)

9. SEEING OUR ATTACHMENTS

As most all military commanders learn, the first step before engaging in any battle (and defeating our attachments is a battle!) is good reconnaissance. Getting pertinent and key information about "the lay of the land." What does the enemy look like? What is the size of, and how formidable is, that opposition? If we have made the Commitment to dealing with our attachments, this is where we must begin our work: sizing up our attachments. We must take the difficult step of opening the door to our attachment warehouse, examining our individual boxes, reading the labels on each box, and ultimately, opening those boxes and emptying out the contents. We need to pause and set aside time to look at the conduct of our life – our thinking, our words, and our actions – and begin to differentiate which are driven by attachment, and which are reflective of our true and better self.

Step 1 – Making the Time
Each of us leads a busy life, filled with responsibilities to fulfill, commitments to complete, and obligations to attend places and events. "Extra time" seems a non-existent luxury. The prospect of taking on one more time demand can seem daunting if not impossible. But that is our first test of our commitment. Working on our attachments will be yet another slice into our schedule. For to begin to see the attachments that we have formed over the cumulative course of our life, we must now allow some new time to pause and search them out – our reconnaissance step.

Ideally on a daily basis, we allot some moments – even if only 15 minutes each day – to look back on our day and reflect upon what happened. This Reflection Period is 15 minutes of time we rarely give ourselves, because we are always "too busy." We are so busy living through each day that we do not take the time truly needed to *manage* and *direct* our day. Instead, we spend our time *reacting* to the demands of the day as dictated by others. Without realizing it, we define most of our life as it is constructed for us by others, all the while believing that we are living a life of our own making. We have become incredibly adept at staying busy, doing the busy-ness of life, such that we forfeit being a little bit busy with our self.

If we truly believe that such a time for reflection cannot be found, that such a priority does not exist for us vis-à-vis the other places we commit ourselves to, then our journey into our attachments is already over before it begins. It is over because we have shown that the first big attachment we have is to "Distraction." We chase other people's unending demands on us (think how important we feel to be so needed!) rather than placing our own well-being as any priority. If we cannot make it past this first step, then our supposed desire to live an unattached life is but a fantasy, not unlike many fantasies that we create in our minds. Fantasies that do not come to pass. So whether this journey is another one of our fantasies – "maybe one of these days" – or an adventure whose time has come, is our choice. A choice that will inherently reflect our attached life.

Step 2 – Doing Our Inventory
So what do we do with this newly set-aside 15 minutes? We pause and review our day. The events that occurred, the thinking that arose, the actions that we took, and the outcomes that resulted. It is not just a chronological review as we might detail in our daily diary. Rather, we reflect on those things that occurred, and use them as a mirror reflecting back at us to identify when and where we moved in attachment.

In such a review, we realize that most of the time we moved almost in a reflex response to events that came our way. We responded with little real thought about what we were doing, but just "did the task" or "engaged in the conversation" sufficiently to complete the event and move on to our next thing. We wander the aisles of the grocery store mindlessly picking up items on our list, oblivious to much of what is happening around us. We start work on our next programming project without much thought about how it will fit into the larger computer system or how it will be used. We argue with a family member without really understanding what she is trying to accomplish or what the motivation is for her decision.

We typically live our life in a kind of rote, robotic haze, usually without understanding why we did what we did, or being aware of how we affected others, or doing one thing while thinking about another, or performing distracted multi-tasking to the detriment of each of those multiple tasks. So in our 15 minutes we try to retroactively see what we *truly* did that day, and what actually drove those actions within us. We look to sort out which actions came out of one of our boxes in our warehouse, and which operated from a less-encumbered source.

Seeing that distinction in our everyday existence is not easy. As said previously, the distinction is often a very fine line that finally gets crossed. So how do we see that distinction in our 15-minute reflection? We look for clues by asking ourselves some of the following questions.

- We look for a somewhat more significant event that stands out within the course of our day.
  Why was it significant to us?

- We look at what we bought today.
  Did we really need it? Why did we need it? Was it a real necessity, or simply a feel-good indulgence?

- We look for the role models that we sought to emulate.
  What were the circumstances in which we sought to emulate someone? Was this a new person to emulate,

or someone we often look back to? Was it an appropriate person to emulate in these circumstances? How did that image affect our handling of the moment?

- We look for any time when we told one of our "old stories" once again.

    What was the story about, and how many times have we told it? Was it new to this audience? Was it pertinent to what the other person(s) was talking about, to the conversation of the moment? Or did we redirect the conversation to our story?

- We look for a frustration or disappointment that we experienced.

    What ambition or aspiration inside of us was thwarted?

- We look for any time we were critical of others, whether we expressed that criticism openly or held it inside.

    What was the expectation we had that they failed to do?

- We look for any time when we felt the need to teach, to correct, to give advice to others.

    What were they doing that we felt needed correcting or teaching? Were we asked to give our opinion? How did the other person respond to our advice?

- We look for any time when others criticized us.

    What did we do to provoke that criticism (whether we believe our conduct was justified or not)? What was our good intention that was criticized instead?

- We look for any time that we projected our perceptions onto others.

    Where did we fail to think about how other people see us, or see a situation, from their vantage point? When did we not stop to consider other scenarios other than just our own? How did we perhaps misread or misinterpret events, or fail to see "the truth"?

- We look for any time that our values, beliefs, honor or integrity were questioned.
  What was being questioned? What did that item mean to our sense of well-being?

- We look for any time that we became angry.
  Regardless of what was done to make us angry, why did we choose to get angry instead of just letting it go?

- We look for any time that we felt fearful, or anxious.
  What was happening to make us feel that way, and what were we feeling fearful of?

- We look for any time that we felt sadness.
  Regardless of what was done to make us sad, why did we choose to get sad instead of just letting it go?

- We look for any time that we experienced joy or happiness.
  What did that happiness feel like? Were we able to appreciate it just in that moment, or did it leave us wanting more of the same, repeated occurrences in the future? Did it make us sad if we realized we had not experienced such joy before?

In essence, in our 15 minutes of reflection we are seeking to identify those moments when our emotional balance went off-center. When it moved into either negative feelings or positive feelings. When we seemed to "be moved" instead of moving. Having made those identifications, then – VERY IMPORTANT – we write them down quickly into our Attachments Journal. Just a simple reminder to ourselves, not a long recap of the event details and their circumstances. We are not writing a dramatic narrative; we already create more than enough drama in our lives all day long! We just jot these reminders down because, over time, we want to see the <u>patterns</u> in which we live our life. Our 1-time events will fall out of the picture; our recurring patterns will begin to stand out, make an impression in our mind, and become ripe for our in-depth work later on. As our Attachments Journal, and thereby our perspective, expands, we will just naturally begin to see our life become a shifting, changing portrait.

<u>Step 3 – Pick An Assisting Friend</u>
When we look into the reflecting mirror of our attachments, the picture we see can likely be quite blurred or distorted. That is because we have spent a lifetime creating our attachments, yet concurrently disguising them from our view. Disguising and distorting them to appear as rational, justifiable thoughts and actions on our part. We have become fully comfortable with them in these altered forms. Seeing through that fog after years of such self-conditioning will require effort, patience, and likely, help.

In the beginning of our efforts, this is where an Assisting Friend may be needed. To help provide a double-check on our observations, our self-reflections. To help us catch ourselves when we find ourselves creating another disguise, another deception over our true motives. To help us see <u>patterns</u> of action, and the potential attachment(s) residing underneath, that is frequently beyond our ability to recognize.

Such an Assisting Friend can come from any source: family member, close friend, social acquaintance, spiritual guide, or professional counselor. But such a Friend must be selected very carefully, using very stringent criteria. An inappropriate selection, however well-intended, can bring more harm to us than good.

Ideally, this is a person who is able to listen to you very deeply, with focused attention without a need to redirect the conversation to his/her own story. A listener who can ask probing, challenging and insightful questions for your own clarity. A person who can speak very frankly but not unkindly with you, with tactful consideration in your sensitive moments. A person who will not try to paper over or minimize what you see in that reflective mirror – you already do enough papering over on your own! Conversely, a person who will also not inflame or exaggerate what you see. A person who will not force you to the Friend's own conclusions. A person who will not tell you what to do; certainly not tell you what *they* would do! A person who can understand what this journey is about, and why you have to take it. A person who will stay with you for an extended time, at least long enough to get you well on your way. A person who will be willing to let you go wherever you need to go in your life as it evolves. And in the end, a person who, if necessary, will be willing to lose you, and their past relationship with you, to what you need to become.

These are very demanding expectations and requirements on your part. But very necessary ones. This is *your* journey, most of which you will have to walk alone to your destination. You cannot afford to have a companion who will seek to take over your journey, or redirect your course, or judge where you wind up. Such an Assisting Friend may prove to be very difficult to find, and several trials may be required.

<u>*Step 4 – Identifying Our Patterns*</u>
As you begin to make your daily postings into your Attachments Journal, this is the initial place where your Assisting Friend can be of help. Perhaps to talk through together the review of the day to help uncover relevant events that you may have skipped over or tended to dismiss. Perhaps to review certain events in a bit more detail to better see how they truly transpired. Perhaps to help see how the event may have unfolded from the perspective of others

rather than your own – the "reflecting perspective" you need rather than just sympathetic handholding or moral / emotional support.

More importantly over the course of time, your Assisting Friend can help you review your Journal entries to find the Patterns that exist in your life. Recurring events and repeated themes, even though the faces and places may change. For example, recurring outcomes of shopping trips. Repeated fights with an individual (family, friend, coworker), or a *type* of adversary or the similar role/position of your adversaries. The frequency of your anger, and any common triggers that seem to be continually present. The ambition(s) that seem to be constantly thwarted by a changing cast of players or circumstances. The repeated criticisms directed your way, or the manner and frequency in which you criticize others. The bouts of sadness, and whether there are repetitive themes to that sadness.

We change our job, sell our house, move to another city, make new friends. Yet after all that appearance of change, within a short time we find ourselves complaining about the same things we were complaining about before all of these moves. The new job now sucks; the new boss doesn't appreciate us; the new house is already inadequate for our needs; our new friends are unsatisfying and do not understand our background experiences. "They" are all new; we are the constant in this picture. Where does the discontent truly lie?

It is by examining the frequency of our patterned actions, and the strength of impact that those actions have upon us, that we are able to differentiate between our wants and our needs. That which we do on occasion is just part of our makeup, perhaps an indulgence which we periodically allow ourselves. They are part of being a human being, and little emotional damage to us is done. Little time and attention should be paid here.

That which we repetitively do – a similar action/reaction with different people or different circumstances – with continuing and significant negative consequences to us even as we nevertheless hold tightly to these patterns of actions, is where attachments are likely to be discovered and explored. Oftentimes, it is only our Assisting Friend who can hold that mirror in front of us to see how our wants have become our attachments.

Most of our days are spent in a blur of busy activity. People, places, events seems to just run together as we constantly move from one event to the next. Consequently, we tend to see these events in the singular – a series of disconnected, one-on-one happenings unrelated to each other. But in reality, our lives and the events that happen to us are very connected. Much of our life is spent in blinded *reaction* and *repetition*, the same scenarios playing out on different stages with different actors playing the same roles opposite our character. But the key to seeing our attachments, our cravings, our loss of self-management, is to see the unconscious repetitive patterns by which we live our life. When we finally see these patterns clearly, without illusion, we can then give up our illusions about the "free choices" we pretend we are making.

Admitting that we have become a prisoner to an artificial life we have created for ourselves, that we in fact are not living the life of free choice as we had thought, can be a devastating realization at first. But it is a necessary realization to begin to find our attachments, reduce or eliminate them, and thereby to allow true happiness to infuse our lives. The adverse events of our life are not the cause of our ongoing unhappiness or personal conflicts. Rather, it is the recurring patterns of our life which entrap us. Patterns constructed by our attachments. Seeing these patterns in action is the road that brings us to the door of our attachment warehouse, and guides us to the appropriate boxes to be unpacked and discarded. And that becomes our next and most difficult step: the unpacking of our boxes of attachments.

10. UNPACKING THE BOXES OF OUR ATTACHMENTS

Step 5 – Expanding Our Reflection Period
As we move further into our process for dealing with our attachments, our Reflection Period becomes ever more important. Our "15 minutes a day" program was a necessary step to get us started, to begin to identify the attachments that we have. But once identified, we need to spend time with them, get to know them more fully, and ultimately change our relationship to them.

To accomplish that, we need to spend more time in our Reflection Period. These periods need to be enveloped in quietness, because seeing our mind, seeing inside the boxes of our attachments, requires a calm and focused effort. A proper time, a proper setting is required.

Each of us has to find the setting that works best for us. Where can we go for the place that calms us, inspires us, makes us feel safe? A chair in our bedroom; a pew in our church; a seat in a meditation hall; a mat in our studio; a rock on a mountainside. We sit quietly, and have a dialog with our mind. We can walk along a beach, or on a forest trail, letting Nature be our comforter, our anchor. We can begin a formal meditation practice, drawing from a variety of meditation styles and disciplines.

The specifics of place and method will vary for each of us. But the requirement is on all of us. We cannot see, and will not hear, the Self that is seeking to present itself to us if we only remain in the chaos and noise of our daily activities. We now have to spend real time with our Self, getting to know our Self in new ways. Quantity time; quality time.

"The quieter you become, the more you can hear."
(Ram Dass, Buddhist teacher)

<u>Step 6 – The Power of "Why"</u>
Once we have seen our patterns, our repetitions, the circumstances that bring us anger or unhappiness, we come back to our attachment warehouse. We go through that front door and look for the box which contains the seeds and trappings of our newly-discovered attachment. But how do we find the right box to open out of so many cartons that stand in front of us? Where is our guide to sort through all of these choices?

Our guide is a Word. In our Attachments Journal we saw What the event was. We saw How we responded. We go to that appropriately-labeled What & How box and take out our box cutter: a one word opener that asks, "Why?" As we open our selected attachment box, each repetition of the word "Why?" lifts one more layer of content out of the box for us to see, to examine. This word slowly, carefully, and deliberately takes us layer by layer deeper into the box, gradually working our way to the very bottom. Each layer we remove contains memories of people we have encountered along Life's way. Words that were said. Actions that occurred. Emotions we felt as a result. Conclusions we drew from the event. Actions we took based upon those conclusions. Actions upon actions upon actions, each action further reinforcing to us the correctness of our conclusions and the events that justified them.

So we wrote in our Attachments Journal What we did: "We went shopping." We wrote How we responded to "shopping": "We bought a new pair of shoes." So we open that box labeled "shopping," and ask <u>Why</u>? "Because I wanted them." <u>Why</u>? – did you need them for something? "No, I just wanted to have them." <u>Why</u>? – has not having them prevented you from doing something you wanted to do? "No. But everyone's wearing this style, and I don't have a pair." Why? did you buy them – just because everyone else has them? "Yes, it makes me feel good about myself." Why? do you need to be stylistically correct and fashionable? "Because it makes me feel successful, like I fit in with others." Why? do you feel you do not fit in well with others, or need to fit in? "Because in school my family couldn't afford to spend much on clothes for us children. So the other girls made fun of me and excluded me." Why? was that important to you? "Because I wanted to be liked by friends in school." Why? "Because I didn't feel liked at home." Why? "Because I was never good enough to be the ballerina my mother herself never became." Why? were you "not good enough"? "Because I hated it, hated all of the practicing, unable to just go out and play with the other kids." Why? did you want to play with the other kids? "Because I was so lonely." Why? did you hate becoming a ballerina? "Because my mother was making me be something besides who I really was, something besides what I wanted to be." Why? did you think you were different than who your mother wanted you to be? "Because I had other talents, other interests, other goals. I wanted to live *my* life, not hers." And what are you doing now? "I work as the Director of a nonprofit performing organization, and I *hate* my job."

So the new shoes make us feel better about ourselves, our life. They are a little salve to a nagging pain inside that will not go away. And if we do not ever actually wear those new shoes, just seeing them sitting in the closet reaffirms to us who we really are deep down. They are a little medallion reminding us of our life-we-wish-we-had, a fantasy that still lives quietly in our mind. A fantasy now covered over in disappointment. All of that from a pair of new shoes, sitting on a shelf at the bottom of our closet.

This is the Power of "Why?" The power of a thousand conversations to be had. It can take us on a long, difficult but fascinating journey if we elect to go. It can guide us like a laser compass to the depths of ourselves, to the dark recesses of our hearts, and layer by layer lighten our load, empty our boxes of attachments. It is a back-and-forth dialog we may have to initially have with our Assisting Friend to get through the early journeys, the first boxes. It is a dialog that will likely not happen in one sitting, versus having one installment, one "Why?" at a sitting; we need a space of time to adapt and assimilate each new layer uncovered. But over time, with practice, the dialog gets easier. It can become more of a "conversation with myself."

These are conversations, once begun, that we will continue to have. That we will be *driven* to have. They are actually never-ending, because there are so many boxes to open, so many layers to reveal. It is a Lifetime journey. But the scope and duration do not dissuade us. It is the dialog itself, the gradual and continuing unfolding of our Self, that is the true reward. It is the walk through the dark places, but coming out in the light of the other side, that keeps us walking and conversing with ourselves. From box to box. From layer to layer. From illusion to truth. From unhappiness to happiness. Because unhappiness can only live in the shadows and confinement of our boxes.

11. CHANGING OUR ATTACHMENTS

"Discernment is a process of letting go what we are not."
(Father Thomas Keating)

We have understood the idea of "attachments" and their negative impact on our happiness. We have looked at examples of the many ways attachments can be created and how they can manifest themselves in our life. We have committed ourselves to reducing the control over our decisions and actions that we have given to our attachments. We have set aside a regular time to pause and review our daily activity in order to see in a new way how our life has been unfolding and reacting. We are recording some significant events of each day, and in regular Reflection Periods – perhaps with an "Assisting Friend" – begun to see the repetitive patterns of our decisions, responses and actions. We have done the hard work of unfolding the layers of our disguised thinking in order to see what has truly driven the course of our life.

Now we have to begin to change those Life patterns. Change how we react to people and events. Empty out our attachment boxes, one at a time, and give up carrying the weight of these heavy loads. We now have to think differently about situations that arise; we now have to act differently to those situations; we now have to operate from a more honest Truth about ourselves than we have ever done before. And we now have to change the direction of our life to move into new places, new people, and new situations that embrace this new Truth.

We now seek to allow ourselves to be happy by no longer allowing ourselves to fail to be happy. We can no longer blame others for our unhappiness; we can no longer expect of others that they will create our happiness for us. We accept that the onus and responsibility for our happiness is on us, not on others. The task seems daunting; the goal seems vague and elusive. How to proceed?

There are a variety of ways we can begin to move into this new thinking, this new way of doing. Each of us has to find the right method(s), the right timing, and the right pacing for him-/herself. The path we take will not be a pre-prescribed series of sequential steps. Our lives and minds do not work that way when we are seeking spiritual and/or personal changes in our way of being. Rather, we explore various methods at once, drawing from each as appropriate in the moment. And we must continually *practice* our changes in order to more fully develop our skills at seeing, understanding, and changing our warehouse of attachments. It is not enough to just see our attachments in our minds; we must *act* in an unattached way.

Step 7 – Prioritizing Our Attachments
We continue maintaining our Attachments Journal and the Reflection Period that we have started. But having begun to see some of the patterns that do exist for us, and how they are affecting us, we now prioritize particular attachments which call out to us for more immediate attention. We cannot tackle at once all of the attachments we begin to discover; there are simply too many, and such a broad-scale effort would diffuse our focus and energy and thereby limit our progress. So we selectively pick and choose. In the beginning, we might select some smaller issues, ones easier for us to look at, requiring simpler changes to effect a difference. These early efforts can serve to sharpen our skills, give us good practice, and build our confidence. As time goes on, our improved skills can allow us to select more difficult challenges, more painful insights, more complex and substantive issues to work with. The appropriate pacing and prioritizing will follow our own natural instincts; we trust our own judgment, and be not in a hurry – this is not a "quick fix" effort. We are not discouraged by the volume of the task; instead, we seek to make much progress on just a few

attachments at a time. Our changes will build upon each other and be cumulative.

Step 8 – Choosing Our Better Responses
In our Reflection Period, we look at each event where the particular attachment arose, we see the outcome(s) that resulted. The way we responded; the way others responded to our response; the back and forth chain of responses that ensued. The pertinent question is, if these were the ways we responded when in attachment, how would we prefer to have responded instead without our attachment in control of us? What are the changes in our patterns that we desire?

Once we have done the analytic work of unpacking the layers of our attachments and see a glimpse of what has been the cause(s) of our actions, only then do we have the opportunity and ability to change our actions. We can now redirect our attachment from an *unhealthy* choice of action to a more *healthy* choice – for all involved. While our ultimate goal may be to eliminate the attachment altogether by emptying the box completely, we can still start off our changes with this redirecting approach. We take back some control of our life by <u>managing</u> our responses, creating new healthy patterns of action, and practicing these new patterns until they become our new reflex. By redirecting our attachments into more positive outcomes, we allow our self-satisfaction, our happiness, to arise in us.

Step 9 – Shortening Our Time Of Recognition
Through our Journaling and Reflection Period, we see not only our patterns that reveal our attachments, but we also begin to see the frequency in which that attachment shows up. The situations that cause it to arise; the manner of our response; the consequences of our response. As we come to know our attachment better, we then look to see it quicker and earlier. We keep that attachment in the

forefront of our mind as we go through the day, not deep in background. Newly sensitized about the old manner of our conduct, <u>we now look to see our attachment arise in the moment it is happening</u> so that we have the opportunity to change its course before any damage is done. The skill to be able to "pause and reflect in the moment," rather than having to reflect after-the-fact, is one of the most important skills for us to develop. And the skill arises out of the quiet time of our daily Reflection Period.

As we recognize an attachment as it is happening, we pause and describe to ourselves in a gentle way what is happening in this moment. What attachment behavior we are evidencing. Then we draw upon our new intended responses that we identified and agreed to during our Reflection Period. We hold the sharpness of our tongue; we reduce our temper; we think about what we will say before we say anything; we buy time – even if but a few seconds – to plan our action before we act; we choose positive tones to speak rather than negative ones; we consider why people are acting as they are so that we can depersonalize their actions; we take back the projections that we are casting upon them of who we believe them to be. We *choose* our desired response, rather than let our attachment reflexively force an undesirable response from us. And we choose the response that will allow happiness for us.

> "Silence was meaningful with the Lakota, and his granting a space of silence before talking was done in the practice of true politeness and regardful of the rule that 'thought comes before speech.' And in the midst of sorrow, sickness, death, or misfortune of any kind, and in the presence of the notable and great, silence was the mark of respect. More powerful than words was silence with the Lakota… As a matter of truth, [the Lakota] was the most sympathetic of men, but his emotions of depth and sincerity were tempered with control… The silent man was ever to be trusted, while the man ever ready with speech was never taken seriously."
> (Chief Luther Standing Bear)

<u>Step 10 – Creating Support Structures</u>
All of this work in redirecting our attachments is solitary, private work. Confusion is often present, discouragement is frequent. So we need to create a structure that will help support our efforts, and keep us motivated and on course. What is typically required is to find a "community" of people who are pursuing similar efforts, who can understand the journey we are making, and with whom they and we can share our experiences. Such a community can be a formal group of some manner, or just a collection of individuals with whom we can relate comfortably. In all likelihood, they will be new people in our life, because we are living a new experience. Conversely, the sad truth is that some individuals that have been in our life may now gradually drop away. These individuals were part of the "you that was," part of our old attachments. Those relationships may not be able to transition with us as we make our own transition.

In addition to community, a new teacher may be required. Someone who has been where we have been and has insights and experiences to share with us. Not a teacher who will overwhelm us with "do this." Instead, someone who can help us see where we now are, and *assist* us (versus tell us) in identifying where we need to go next. In our state of being in an unsure flux, it can be easy to simply transfer a new attachment to this teacher, a teacher who seems like a rock of stability vis-à-vis our unstable state. We need to examine this closely to ensure that this is a <u>separate</u> relationship between both teacher and student, not a new self-serving, idealized projection for either. This "teacher" can be a spiritual director or a psychological counselor, whichever is more comfortable for us given our individual background and way of seeing the world. But another caution: there are those spiritualists and counselors who attempt to blend these two perspectives together. However well-intended, this blending is not advisable and should be avoided. Follow a personal spiritual path; or follow a psychological counseling path. They are two different routes, but each can arrive at the same destination.

Lastly, we need to avail ourselves of the relevant literature. The writings in this realm of change are extensive. There can be great wisdom in such readings, comfort in these different stories, with respect to the struggles we are experiencing. They can provide potential insight and guidance for our next steps. And such readings can be re-accessed periodically to refresh our understandings of their insights. But as with selecting an individual teacher, we need to read with discernment and caution. One person's experience in working with attachments, one person's perspective, may or may not be "true," or may or may not be applicable to where you are and where you need to go next.

Step 11 – Eliminating Attachments

"Managing" our attachments, as described above, may prove to be sufficient for many of our desires to reduce conflict and eliminate much negativity in our life. It may be especially effective given the realities of the time and energy we may have available to devote to this effort in light of our current circumstances.

At some point, though, we may determine that our commitment is strong enough, or our need is so powerful, or a particular attachment is so dominating, that we need to *eliminate* it altogether. This is no easy task, although the work we have done to date will serve us well as a good starting point. Though we may be able to delve very deeply inside a particular attachment box on our own, it is very unlikely that we can arrive at that final bottom, empty those final contents, without outside assistance. Specifically, trained assistance.

Eliminating attachments is a long-term effort, though interim benefits will be realized along the way. It takes much time because we are attempting to reach that final layer at the bottom of our attachment box, and there are simply many layers to be unpacked. There will be much pain re-experienced from past hurts, perhaps devastating hurts. There will be "darker thoughts" in our minds that must be encountered and admitted to. It is not enough to just intellectually retell "our story." We have to once again *see* those images that we have kept so carefully packed away. We have to *re-feel* and *re-experience* the emotions we felt in those past moments. We then have to acknowledge how we would like to *re-write* the script of our actions – what we *wished* we had done, what we *should* have done, instead of what we did. We have to *say* now what we wanted to say then. We have to release the experience out of the *body* – from the muscles, veins and bones where we have physically stored the intense energy of our experience. We have to revisit the *conclusions* that we drew at the time, and the *life decisions* we made based upon those conclusions – the directions we set, the patterns of thinking that we formed. And from these new insights and understandings, we have to create a new plan, a new direction, for our life.

As these darker sides of our Self are exposed, they can send us into temporary tailspins. But there is no avoiding these inner truths about our Self if we are to arrive at a more complete and lasting inner peace. And to be sure, once we pass through and survive this storm – and survive it we will – the effort will prove worth it. There is a great burden to be lifted, a lightness in living to be had, a true and honest connection with Life than has been experienced before. It is a journey that requires proper preparation. It is a great effort; it is a great reward. It is not a journey for everyone, and that is OK.

"To willingly reside in our distress,
no longer resisting what is,
is the real key to transformation.
As painful as it may be to face our deepest fears,
we do reach the point where
it's more painful not to face them.
This is a pivotal point in the practice life."
(Ezra Bayda, "Bursting the Bubble of Fear")

12. OVERCOMING RESISTANCES

"Being unattached to things does not mean that you do not care about them nor do you not interact with them. On the contrary, you should care very much about them. You care that such things are allowed to be just what they truly are, not what you would have them to be. And you do not cede the power to them to tell you how you will be, or think, or act. In such mutual freedom of love for what each thing is, each is able to fulfill and express exactly what their true inner nature is. You are unattached to outside things, but you are not uncaring, unconcerned, or unconnected with them."

(Lesson 61, *Lessons From The Teacher Buddha*)

In pursuing our efforts to remove the force of attachment from our lives, we will encounter wonderful periods of a new sense of freedom. Periods of less negative feelings. Periods of less stress and more control over our actions. But we will also experience periods of doubt about making this effort, hesitancy about what may come out of it, or frustration at our inconsistency or flagging commitment. These are all very natural experiences. We will take a number of steps backwards in our journey through our Attachment Warehouse, but we will always come back to the journey and continue to move forward overall. Any progress we make will be progress that benefits us; those benefits will never be lost.

Losing Our Passion
We may harbor fears that if we lose our attachments, and the driving force in us that our attachments provoke, then we will also lose our passion, the motivation for doing what we do. We are taught that passion is a good thing, and that we should seek out and discover our passions in life. "Follow your passion" is often offered as a guide to finding our direction. This is all true – up to a point. Following passions created from our attachments will most certainly guide us into <u>unhappiness</u>. False passions, driven by selfish need rather than unselfish giving, will ultimately drive us into continuing conflict with our larger community, with the realities of Life. *Reducing our attachments will only reduce our passion for false things.* But it will open a new door for our passions towards what is real, what is in our truest interests. That kind of passion does exist, and that is the true passion we look for and to now follow.

Loss Of Self
We often believe that the things that we are attached to are the very things that define who we are – *our Self.* Our attachment objects, our toys, our beliefs *are* us. If we give away these attachments, we feel as though we are giving away our own Self, our very essence. The meaning of the experiences of our life. The very things that make us a unique human being. Taking that away, what is left? *Who* is left?

We are not our attachments. We are more than our attachments. We have a core, a substance, that is never lost no matter how much we may cover over and disguise it. That core self may be unfamiliar to us now, but it has always been here with us. By losing our attachments we are not taking on someone new; we are instead welcoming back an old friend, our best friend. Our Self. Our attachments may have molded a new face over our original form, but it only did so to *protect* that original form, not to hide it in supposed ugliness. That is the true Self that we seek to find, set free, and let live fully on its own. As the Biblical teachings tell us, we must first lose our (false) self in order to find our (true) Self. Finding, meeting, and revealing that hidden Self – the unfamiliar stranger that we know so well – is the true excitement for making this journey.

New Forms Of Attachment
Attachments are devilish things. They can be redirected or lessened. But oftentimes it may feel like once we deal with one attachment, another shows up. Or multiple objects or actions seem to spring out of the same box. It can feel like a game of whack-a-mole: as fast as we deal with one experience, another quickly arises in its place. We can become exhausted from this never-ending effort.

This is where our resolve to continue on will be tested. As we are able over time to see the commonality of our cravings, and the connections to a similar source, the more we will be able to reduce the multiple expressions that arise. There will be a multiplier effect: the more connections we see, the more of our attachments will be concurrently dealt with. It is not the total count on our attachment scorecard that is most important; it is seeing how the attachment process works, and becoming skilled at detaching ourselves, that really matters. Given the vast potential of our mind to bedevil us, dealing with attachment becomes a natural part of our daily life, a continuing line item on our to-do list.

Concerns About Becoming Uncaring
Losing our attachments to things and people (detaching), reducing or redirecting our passions, can sound as though we no longer care about our world. No longer concerned about people and their circumstances. No longer willing to be involved with our family or community. Such uncaring would feel as a total misdirection to

the spiritual values and community responsibilities we have been taught. So we may be very reluctant to going down a road that might lead us to an uncaring, disconnected existence.

Once again, our fears are understandable but unwarranted. Living without attachment does not mean living without connection, without engagement. Quite the opposite; it means that our connections are even stronger, because they are no longer built upon selfish motivations and unrealistic expectations. Our relationships are now built upon *honesty*, and a true desire to give *without expecting reward*. It means having the love to take others *just as they are*. It means living *with* others, not living to remake others. This is the highest form of caring, of being with others. The opportunity to live without attachment should be a positive force pulling us to it, not a negative barrier driving us away from an unattached life.

> Q: "How can you [experience life, all the good emotions, all the bad ones] if you're detached?"
>
> A: "Detachment doesn't mean you don't let the experience *penetrate* you. On the contrary, you let it penetrate you *fully*. That's how you are able to leave it."
>
> "… If you hold back on the emotions --- if you don't allow yourself to go all the way through them --- you can never get to being detached, you're too busy being afraid… By throwing yourself into these emotions, by allowing yourself to dive in, all the way, over your head even, you experience them fully and completely. You know what pain is. You know what love is. You know what grief is. And only then can you say, 'All right. I have experienced that emotion. I recognize that emotion. Now I need to detach from that emotion for a moment.'"
>
> (Morrie Schwartz, *Tuesdays with Morrie*, by Mitch Albom.)

Resistance From Others

When we move from an attached life to an unattached life, we change. Our thinking changes. Our decisions change. Our reactions change. Our interactions with others change. Our life's direction changes. Change – however scary that may be at times – is why we moved onto this road in the first place.

The place where we were was a place created by our attachments. The place where we are going is a place created by non-attachment. They are not the same place; they are not compatible. The people and structures in our old attached life will not live in our new unattached life. We are moving. Will others be able to move alongside us to our new place?

We are very likely to encounter resistance, perhaps strong resistance if not outright attempted sabotage, to the new Self that is being revealed. As we were attached to other things, some of those things were equally attached to us; it was a mutual attachment for each. If we are now seeking to become unattached, to live more freely, those who were attached to us but are not seeking to change can fight us every step of our way. By our own example, we threaten their desire to stay in their status quo. They may attack our new values, question our new thinking, be suspicious of our new actions, assert their disapproval of the new risks we are taking. They may take our changes very personally as an implied attack on <u>them</u>. So they may well put in our path one barrier after another as they sense our old relationship progressively slipping away.

The choice is ours. And it is an important choice. We can stop our efforts and give in to their objections. We can try to reassure these old relationships, try to help them depersonalize our changes relative to them, but this is likely to be to no avail. Or we can continue on, being respectful to others but undaunted in our travels, accepting that some relationships will simply not survive.

Should not survive, given their unhealthiness. It is a very difficult choice, likely a painful break to undergo. But in some circumstances it may be a necessary one.

What will offset the difficulty of this painfulness is the supportive people who will begin to appear to sustain and encourage us. Some will come from existing relationships, some of whom may have suffered in the past from being our objects of attachment; they will be just as happy to be out from under the weight of our craving attachments. Some will be admirers of our courage and stimulated to start their own journey alongside us. And some will be entirely new players, welcomed by the new openness that we have made available to them.

Separating from existing relationships is never easy. But we do it necessarily many times over in the course of our lifetime. Separation from parents, from siblings, from school friends, from early lovers, from co-workers, from adult friends. Increasingly from spouses; inevitably from our children. Some relationships end; some keep up and get transformed into new ways of being. It is all part of life's cycle. When the time comes, it is a change that must be embraced in order to live a full, complete and maturing life. When we allow these relationships to change when they naturally occur and as they naturally must, we allow the fuller happiness which awaits us to permeate our life.

13. LIVING WITHOUT ATTACHMENTS

> "When you are able to move beyond your False Self—at the right time and in the right way—*it will feel precisely as if you have lost nothing.* In fact, it will feel like freedom and liberation. When you are connected to the Whole, you no longer need to protect and defend the mere part. You are now connected to something inexhaustible."
> (Fr. Richard Rohr)

Attachments can come from many causes, from many sources of experiences in our life. They will manifest themselves and affect each of us differently. They affect all of us, regardless of our age, circumstances or position in society. They are with us in some form, to some degree, our entire life. We can progressively reduce them, keep them in check, through our willingness to encounter them directly and see the falsity in them, and the truth in us. Yet even with our most dedicated efforts, we do not simply go from "being attached" to "being unattached"; it is a progressive, gradual change that we make over our lifetime, with increasing benefits gained each step of the way. It is realizing and acknowledging those growing benefits that keep us moving forward in this pursuit in spite of the periodic discouragements. What is required to make this journey is making this an ever-present priority in our Life's goals and the way we live. It is in the making of that journey that we allow happiness to come into our life, replacing the many forms of unhappiness that we are tempted towards.

In the March 2014 edition of "O Magazine," Oprah Winfrey talks about her most prized possession: her custom-made bathtub hand-carved in Italy from a solid piece of onyx, made uniquely for her. In the remodeling of her house, this was the one item she found she just could not part with, even though it no longer fit with her redesign plan. She could certainly afford to get another tub that would fit her new bathroom décor. Why was she hanging on so tightly to keeping this tub, even though it no longer fit the place to where her life had now come?

Near tears, she gave the order to the work team to pull the tub out and move forward. Mind seemingly overruling heart. It was two months later before she finally asked herself what that tub represented to her. And the answer came: it represented wealth. "I've truly made it." As a child growing up she had had anything but wealth, and had little apparent prospect of ever having any. But after years of hard work and a "willingness to try," she had long since arrived at a pinnacle of show business – and life – success. Yet it was her long-seeded insecurities from poverty and a difficult life that gave her a Craving to hang on to that tub, just to keep convincing herself that it was all real.

Oprah went on to say, "For sure, the tub had become my symbol of success. For some people it might be shoes and handbags, square footage, where your children attended school. For me it was a tub … Releasing that tub opened me to all the changes that have come since. I literally raised the roof, gutted the kitchen, and brought in more light. Which, come to think of it, is a poignant metaphor for my new life."

Allow yourself the happiness that you deserve.

> "There where clinging to things ends,
> there God begins to be."
> (Meister Eckhart, German theologian)

14. AUTHOR AND PUBLICATIONS

Randy Bell lives in the mountains of western North Carolina. He is a life-long student of spirituality as well as American history who spent 30 years in higher education as a teacher, administrator, and independent management consultant to colleges and universities across the United States. He is currently the founder and Director of Spring Creek Spirituality for spiritual training, has written eleven books, and writes two blogs on a variety of spiritual and social commentary topics. He is a member of the North Carolina Writer's Network and Spiritual Directors International.

Other publications by Randy Bell available from www.McKeeLearningFoundation.com

Books:
God and Me: A Statement of Belief
    ISBN-13: 978-0-9710549-5-0

Lessons from the Teacher Jesus
    ISBN-13: 978-0-9710549-2-9

Lessons from the Teacher Buddha
    ISBN-13: 978-0-9710549-7-4

Lessons from the Teacher Moses
    ISBN-13: 978-0-9710549-8-1

Lessons from the Teacher Muhammad
    ISBN-13: 978-0-9710549-9-8

Buddhism: An Introductory Guide
ISBN-13: 978-0-9710549-1-2

Starting A Personal Meditation Practice
ISBN-13: 978-0-9895428-0-7

Forms of Meditation: Methods and Practices
for Contemplation and Prayer
ISBN-13: 978-0-9710549-6-7

The Seven Virtues of a Spiritual Life
ISBN-13: none

Career Choices For Your Soul
ISBN-13: 978-0-9710549-4-3

Executive's Guidebook for Institutional Change
ISBN: 0-9710549-0-8

Blog Commentaries:

Thoughts From The Mountain
www.ThoughtsFromTheMountain.blogspot.com

A social commentary from a spiritual and ethical perspective.

Our Spiritual Way
www.OurSpiritualWay.blogspot.com

Supporting personal commitment, individual insight,
and listening to guidance
as we share our spiritual journeys together.

www.ingramcontent.com/pod-product-compliance
Lightning Source LLC
Chambersburg PA
CBHW022155080426
42734CB00006B/450